T0208711

BEFORE IT'S TOO LATE

A Parent's Guide on Teens, Sex, and Sanity

SHEILA OVERTON, MD
With Treacy Colbert

Before It's Too Late
A Parent's Guide on Teens, Sex, and Sanity

Copyright © 2010 by Sheila Overton, MD.

iUniverse rev. date: 3/8/2016
Author rev. date: 3/8/2016

All rights reserved. No part of this book may be used or reproduced by any means, graphic, electronic, or mechanical, including photocopying, recording, taping or by any information storage retrieval system without the written permission of the author except in the case of brief quotations embodied in critical articles and reviews.

iUniverse books may be ordered through booksellers or by contacting:

iUniverse
1663 Liberty Drive
Bloomington, IN 47403
www.iuniverse.com
1-800-Authors (1-800-288-4677)

Because of the dynamic nature of the Internet, any Web addresses or links contained in this book may have changed since publication and may no longer be valid. The views expressed in this work are solely those of the author and do not necessarily reflect the views of the publisher, and the publisher hereby disclaims any responsibility for them.

ISBN: 978-1-4502-5366-6 (sc)
ISBN: 978-1-4502-5367-3 (e)

Print information available on the last page.

In Loving Memory of Mamo

and

For My Parents
Ed and Marilyn Overton

Hmmm! Teenagers.
They think they know everything.
You give them an inch, and they swim all
over you.

— Sebastian, "The Little Mermaid"

ACKNOWLEDGEMENTS

The creation of *Before It's Too Late* has been a labor of love. The nearly two-and-a-half years it has taken to research, write, and publish this book has stretched my imagination, physical stamina, and intellect in ways I could never have predicted. And, I could never have accomplished this task without the guidance and support of many people along the way.

I want to express my deep gratitude to each of the following individuals who contributed to *Before It's Too Late:*

Ruth Stroud and Jeff Graham, for listening to my vision for the book, reading the original material, and encouraging me to go forward with my dreams. You are dear friends whom I will always treasure.

Christine Rodgerson, for being in the right place at the right time. You listened to my hopes for this book, reviewed my original proposal, and had the foresight to recommend my collaborative writer, Treacy Colbert. And, you offered encouragement as a friend and mentor.

My mother, Marilyn Overton, for your support in taking the time to read so much of my initial work, to offer feedback, insight, and expertise that only a former English teacher could provide. You are a very supportive, loving mother, and you and Dad are a major reason for the success that all your children have achieved. We love you.

To all my family and dear friends who took time from their busy schedules to review chapters and to offer perspective, including my incredibly loving sister, Marsha Dodson, my lovely sister-in-law, Nancy Overton, my amazing cousin, Carolyn Samiere, and my ever-so-dear friends of many years Terese Brookins, DDS, MPH; Toby Brock, RN; Nafisa Abdullah, MD; and my new friends Shauna Kurodo, RN, and Donna Krenz, RN.

Friends and family members understood what I was trying to accomplish with this book, and helped in searching out contact people, answering questions, big and small, and offering support. These include my darling youngest sister Renee Watson, my wonderful sister-in-law Jeanne Overton, and my dear friends LaTonya Botshekan, CNM, and Harold Sylvester.

To my colleagues who served on the Kaiser Permanente West Los Angeles Teen Pregnancy and STD Prevention Program, it was a precious honor to serve as your chair. Each of you volunteered your time, lent your expertise, and gave from your hearts to the hundreds of teens and parents that we served for over a decade. I thank you so very much: Margie Bell, RN; LaTonya Botshekan, CNM; Karen Bratman, LCSW; Toby Brock, RN; Gwen Brown, RN; Adrienne Bullock, LVN; Dawn Cashe, MD; Linda Cruise, LVN; Erique Emel, MD; Tracy L. Fietz, R.N.P., M.S., Medical Group Administrator; Shelly Johnson, RN; Sharon Jones, MD; Fatemeh Khaghani, RN, EdD; Annette Neumann, RN; Mathias Schar, MD; Kym Taylor, PA; and Ramon Yera, MD.

To all the parents and teens who attended our seminars, thank you for your participation and for the feedback that you so generously gave.

To my collaborative writer, Treacy Colbert, it's hard to know where to begin. You are extraordinarily talented and have served as a shining light for me throughout this process. I am so very thankful to have had someone with your amazing intellect, grace, wisdom, and knowledge to guide me on this journey. I am proud of and honored by the work that we have done together. I could not have completed this project without you and will never be able to fully express my appreciation for all that you have done.

To my children, Jarin and Gabrielle. I love you dearly and am very proud of your accomplishments and the thoughtful and centered ways you are living your lives. I look forward, with great anticipation, to watching you both achieve your dreams and beyond.

Last, but not least, to my husband and life partner, Greg. You have always been my biggest fan and most ardent supporter, and that held true while I wrote this book. In many ways, it's been a selfish pursuit, requiring countless hours of work. You allowed me the time I needed and you never once complained. You read chapters, offered insight and perspective, gave constructive feedback, and more. I love you and thank you for all the support and love you have given me, not just during this project, but always.

I send my love and best wishes to everyone mentioned above. To anyone I may have failed to mention, please accept my gratitude.

TABLE OF CONTENTS

INTRODUCTION

Most parents will admit to at least some apprehension when it comes to guiding their children about sexual health. *Before It's Too Late, A Parent's Guide on Teens, Sex, and Sanity,* addresses this issue. It provides parents with practical information and advice they can use to help direct their teens. This is crucially important because:

- The U.S. has one of the highest teen pregnancy rates in the industrialized world.

- Teen pregnancy alters lives irrevocably, abruptly curtailing youth and frequently hurling families into chaos.

- There are staggering rates of sexually transmitted diseases (STDs)* among U.S. teens; several million per year. This amounts to a major public health crisis.

Before It's Too Late offers a uniquely fresh approach for parents to lower their anxiety and fears about teens and sex. It is written from my perspective as an obstetrician/gynecologist, who has practiced since 1987, and as the mother of two. I have worked passionately in the area of teen pregnancy and STD prevention, chairing a major Los Angeles hospital-based Teen Pregnancy and STD Prevention Program for over a decade. My professional involvement with and care of teen girls whose lives have been forever changed by teen pregnancy or who were horrified to learn that they had contracted an STD continues to compel me.

Parents are the front-line defense in preventing teen pregnancy and STDs; however, they can't do it alone. *Before It's Too Late* will supplement the efforts of educators, health care professionals, policymakers, and others in achieving this goal. A dizzying maze of information exists about teens and sex. This book simplifies the information and educates parents with concrete, medically accurate information, positive tips, interactive tools, and specific advice that they can use to help their teens avoid becoming another teen pregnancy or STD statistic.

Knowing how to talk to kids about sex is important, but it's not nearly enough. *Before It's Too Late* covers timely topics from current teen sex behavior, the life-changing impact of teen pregnancy, the unique contraceptive issues for teens, the life-threatening consequences of STDs contracted by teens and how to prevent them, the issues surrounding school-based sex education, the most effective ways for parents to communicate with and to guide their teens, and where to turn for additional assistance. *Before It's Too Late* educates parents on these crucial topics, step-by-step, and reaffirms their instinctive ability to communicate with their teens.

Parents will finish this book with a new and powerful language to use in communicating with their teens, a richly positive and practical, knowledge-based approach, and an improved ability to guide their teens toward healthy, responsible, and values-based decision making about their sexual health.

* I use the term sexually transmitted diseases (STDs) throughout this book, because this is the term most parents recognize. Medical journal articles generally refer to sexually transmitted infections, or STIs. The terms are interchangeable.

* The National Campaign to Prevent Teen Pregnancy has been changed to The National Campaign to Prevent Teen and Unplanned Pregnancy. Both titles are used interchangeably in this book

** Names and identifying details are changed to protect identity in the following chapters.

Chapter 1

Protecting Your Teen: Sharpening Skills for a New Phase

There are only two lasting bequests we can hope to give our children. One of these is roots, the other, wings.

—Hodding Carter

I wrote *Before It's Too Late: A Parent's Guide on Teens, Sex, and Sanity* to help you, as parents, protect your teens from pregnancy and sexually transmitted diseases (STDs) and to help you guide them toward healthy, responsible, and values-based decisions about sex. My deep passion about stemming the tide of teen pregnancy and the epidemic of STDs among teens is at the core of this book.

Serving as chairperson of the Teen Pregnancy Prevention Program at a large metropolitan hospital for over 10 years allowed me to better understand the level of concern and anxiety so many parents have about teen sex, pregnancy, and STDs. I listened as they shared their desires for more programs that bring parents and teens together to discuss the challenges parents face in guiding their children about sex. I witnessed the empowerment they experienced right before my eyes after participating in exercises designed to improve their parenting skills in this area.

I am reminded of the yearning parents have for accurate and practical advice on this subject, and of their frequent despair about not feeling up to the task from an article about a male TV star in a popular women's magazine. As I read his article, "My Family Life," I was struck by a portion of his response to a tricky question from one of his kids: "The other day [my daughter] asked me about the birds and the bees—indirectly. I felt like I was drowning. What a dope!"

Sound familiar?

Later that evening, I watched a vibrant, veteran female talk show host interviewing pregnant teens. This host, so skilled at communicating with others, confessed that she had never really talked to her own daughter about sex during her teen years. This highly skilled professional, despite all her training and experience, was just like so many parents—she may have found that aspect of parenting easier to ignore or replace with wishful thinking.

Talking to tweens and teens about sex—it can bring otherwise confident, assertive, successful, and powerful people to their knees. I've witnessed this scenario over and over again in my career as a physician who emphasizes teen pregnancy and STD prevention.

In my experience, very few people feel confident in their ability to talk to and educate their teens about sex, pregnancy, and STDs. Even some of my wonderful, highly skilled professional colleagues have expressed near panic when their child became a tween or teen, and they realized that they didn't know what to say about sex or how to say it. This kind of reaction is mirrored in parents from all walks of life; from experienced executives who supervise large teams of people and service workers who regularly communicate with all kinds of customers, to stay-at-home moms who are top volunteers. They all share the same uneasiness about talking with their kids about sex.

As a parent, not only do I have empathy, but I can say, "I've been there too" in dealing with the angst and complexities surrounding this critical task.

As a physician, I know that you, as parents, definitely possess the basic skills you need to protect your kids and to effectively guide them about this very important topic. These basic skills, however, need to be refreshed with up-to-date knowledge about teen sexual health, improved communication know-how, and a decidedly positive attitude. By the time you finish this book, you'll have the tools you need to be full participants in successfully and proactively parenting your teens. Where you once felt insecure, you'll become confident, and what once seemed like an awkward conversation will be transformed into highly effective communication.

Preventing teen pregnancy and STDs and raising sexually healthy children requires frequent, ongoing conversations about sex, and consistent pointers and reminders. Unfortunately, too many parents evade this task. The magnitude of parental reluctance to discuss sex with their kids was highlighted in a survey in which the vast majority of parents of 10- to 12-year-old children attending focus groups felt that they should talk to their children about sex, but many had not done so. The two top barriers reported by these parents were feeling uncomfortable and thinking that someone else would be better at it.

Another survey concluded that many parents and teens do not talk about sex before the kids engage in sex. This information reflects the large communication divide that too often exists between parents and teens.

Parents—it's not enough to keep your fingers crossed about your teens and sex. Not only can you have a huge impact on teen sexual health and prevention of teen pregnancy and STDs, but you can't afford not to. You'll learn more about the consequences of teen sex, pregnancy, and STDs in upcoming chapters.

Remember that you're not alone if you feel cautious or nervous about talking with your teens about sex. Remember, too, that this isn't the first time you've felt uncertain about a parenting issue. As an obstetrician, I've had a bird's-eye view of parenting concerns that arise as soon as the bundle of joy arrives.

First-time parents especially crave information about infant care. They're not sure if their baby is getting enough milk, sleeping too much or too little, peeing or pooping enough, and much more. New mothers often find that breastfeeding doesn't come as naturally as they thought and require much assistance and support.

With help from caring family members and health care providers, new moms and dads gradually learn what's normal and what's not, what to watch out for, and how to competently care for their newborn. These parents already possessed the basic intuition and skills necessary to provide for their newborn; they just needed additional knowledge, support, and guidance.

Just as moms and dads achieve successful parenting of their infants, they also effectively guide their children through many subsequent phases. Sometimes, parental instinct may have been all that was needed. However, at other times outside advice or further education or research was necessary.

Consider just a few of the milestones that you have helped your child reach:

- Mastering toilet training

  OK, this may have been your least favorite task. No doubt, it took plenty of patience and persistence.

- Learning basic safety awareness

  You taught your children not to play in the streets, never to accept a ride from strangers, and to always wear seat belts. These required setting clear rules, as well as explaining the harm that can occur if these rules are broken.

- Riding a bicycle

  Many parents take tremendous pride and joy in helping their child attain this skill. The mastery of this task often leads to a closer parent/child bond.

- Handling childhood skirmishes and disappointments

  Teaching children to handle conflict and unhappy situations in life is critical to their achieving emotional health. This requires emotional insight on the part of parents. Sometimes, assistance from school counselors or other professionals may be needed.

- Understanding the dangers of tobacco, underage alcohol use, and illegal drug use

  This requires education by parents as well as supervision and vigilance. School programs such as DARE and health care provider-led discussions can complement and support parental efforts.

In each of these tasks and in so many others, you have shown your ability to teach, protect, and demonstrate concern and love for your child. In the same way and by incorporating many of the same principles, you can also successfully guide your child through today's very challenging sexual landscape. As with every other task, there will be difficult and trying times, but also rewarding and bonding experiences. There may be times when you'll wish you had a 24-hour camera to monitor your child, but the options in this book will help you eliminate that type of thinking.

The key is to approach the task of sex education for your child with the same assurance you had when handling other parenting tasks in your child's life. You needed to be patient and persistent, set clear expectations and rules, share pride, joy, and emotional intimacy, supervise and be ever-vigilant, and seek outside resources and support when needed. I'll reinforce how to do that throughout the book.

Along with relaxing a bit and realizing that you've already mastered core parenting skills and can use many of these same skills when it comes to sex education, I also urge you to develop and to express an attitude of optimism. What does optimism have to do with teens and sex? The answer is plenty, and here's why.

The teen years are often feared as difficult, tumultuous, and trying. It's as if this phase is something that parents can thank their lucky stars if they "survive." I know the teen years are not totally blissful or stress-free, but despite some of the difficulties that go along with this phase in your child's life, you can choose to approach your tweens and teens from a point of view that reflects optimism. Simply put, this means expecting positive behaviors and outcomes and creating the kind of atmosphere that promotes them.

After all, more often than not, our tweens and teens bring great joy to our lives. Whether they're excelling academically, in sports, or the arts, or demonstrating loyalty to their friends and family, how often have you felt pride?

Too often, we focus on teens as people "at risk." They are at risk for getting into trouble, using drugs, doing less than admirably in school, having sex, or getting pregnant, etc. What if that mind-set were changed and teens were expected to achieve academically, develop their interests, pursue their passions, serve their community, and avoid peer pressure to engage in early and/or risky sexual behavior?

So many teens make positive contributions to our world. They volunteer to serve the needy; represent their schools and communities in academic contests, sporting events, and artistic endeavors; collect money to aid those affected by natural disasters, and much more.

By viewing our teens through a prism of optimism, we set high expectations. When it comes to sex, this means envisioning that our children will listen to our advice, resist sexual pressure from peers, respect themselves, and think as well as act responsibly. In a broader sense, it can mean that we can trust that our teens will see the vast opportunities they have to succeed in life and work toward realizing their goals.

This optimism also extends to your attitude toward your ability to be effective parents. Remember, you have already demonstrated your competence in parenting in other areas. The skills needed to educate your child about sex are very similar to the skills you used to oversee other important tasks and achievements. You can and must believe in yourselves, just as you believe in your teen. This sentiment is beautifully summed up here.

> *We must return optimism to our parenting,*
> *to focus on the joys, not the hassles;*
> *the love, not the disappointments;*
> *the common sense, not the complexities.*
>
> —Fred G. Gosman

Unlike the actor who felt like he was "drowning" at the prospect of talking with his daughter about sex, you'll have the information in *Before It's Too Late* to help you brave these waters with a sense of trust in your basic ability to successfully parent your child with enhanced knowledge, improved communication skills, and a positive, optimistic outlook.

Chapter 2

Teen Sexual Behavior: Changes and Challenges

Adolescence is a period of rapid changes. Between the ages of 12 and 17, for example, a parent ages as much as 20 years.

—Unknown

When it comes to teens and sex, as parents we tend to allow fear and worry to interfere with our understanding of the issues and our ability to proactively guide our children. We also underestimate the huge difference we can make in positively influencing our children's attitudes and behavior. We have more power than we might realize—teens surveyed continually identify their parents as most influential in their decisions about sex. To help you wield that influence effectively, this chapter describes what you need to know about current teen sexual attitudes and behavior. With this information, you'll be less likely to duck into denial by thinking "my child doesn't do that," or "my child would never do that," and be better prepared to talk with and guide your teen calmly and honestly.

What's Changed?

How much has really changed since you were a teen? A minority of today's parents were a part of the 1960s sexual revolution. Slogans from that period included "Free Love" and "Make Love, Not War." Compared with that era, the sexual climate for today's teens may actually be more subdued. A recent article in a prominent U.S. newspaper confirmed this view, stating, "today's teenagers are more conservative about sex than previous generations."

So what has changed? According to the most recent National Youth Risk Behavior Survey of ninth to 12th grade students, fewer students report they "ever had sexual intercourse" today compared to 1991. Does this mean that we need to be less concerned about teen sex behavior? The answer is that parents have plenty to be concerned about. As we'll learn, teen pregnancy and STD rates are staggering and the need for alarm remains high.

Parents must also take care to keep abreast of the significant transformation that has occurred in our society, especially since they were teens. We now have more displays of sex in the media and more explicit music lyrics. Hip-hop songs like "I Can Tell You Wanna F—" by 504 Boyz are commonplace. Our kids have new gadgets to transmit and view more sexual material (cell phones, iPods, video games, personal computers). And, we have a greater acceptance of unmarried sex and out-of-wedlock births in our communities.

What hasn't changed, however, are the hopes and dreams parents have for their children, and the worries they have about them. The columnist Ellen Goodman tapped into this sentiment: "The central struggle of parenthood is to let our hopes for our children outweigh our fears."

This is also my hope for you as you read this chapter. You will learn much about current teen sex attitudes and behavior. This information will allow you not only to become a better prepared parent, but a more empowered one.

Before It's Too Late

Despite what our teens might have us believe, as parents we are good for more than money and food. Our ability to clearly and consistently voice our values, our willingness to listen to our teens, and our vigilance in calmly and honestly describing the behavior we expect all profoundly influence our teens, eye-rolling and sighs notwithstanding. Think back on your own experience as a teen. Were there rules or boundaries you deeply resented at the time? Did you later grudgingly accept that maybe your parents were right or even feel thankful that they placed limitations on you? Or you may have had the opposite experience, where no parent was available to guide you, especially where sex was concerned. If that was true in your case, you now have the opportunity with your teen to offer the direction and safety net you didn't have.

Trends in Teen Sex

As noted, fewer teens are having sexual intercourse than they were in 1991, when the YRBS (Youth Risk Behavior Survey) began, and fewer say they have had sexual intercourse with four or more persons. That's the good news. However, although teen sex has declined since 1991, a majority of 12th grade high school students report that they have had sexual intercourse.

A closer look at the ages of teens who are having sex gives us reason to pay careful attention. It's not uncommon for ninth-graders, who are usually 14 years old, to report on the YRBS that they have had sex. This is cause for concern for many reasons, one of which is the lack of emotional maturity needed to handle an intimate sexual relationship at this age.

As parents, we need to be aware that the younger a teen girl is when she has sex, the more likely it is that the sex was involuntary. And, the younger a teen girl is when she starts having sex, the more likely she is to end up having more sexual partners. Clearly, teens having sex is risky behavior—and very young teens having sex is even more so. A small percentage of kids younger than 13 report having had sex. A child younger than 13 is just that—a child. When a child younger than 13 has sex, this behavior is more likely to be a clue to the presence of other serious problems such as family dysfunction or drug use.

Of the teens that I have cared for, those who reported initiating sex at ages 12 to 13 almost always admitted to using drugs and/or alcohol. Many of them came from unstable home environments and were involved in the criminal justice system. What I want to emphasize here is that sexual intercourse among very young teens is often associated with other social problems that require attention.

9

As in the adult population, a percentage of teens define themselves as lesbian, gay, bisexual, or transgender (LGBT). There is increased risk of STD transmission in this population. Specifically, there is significant concern about male-to-male transmission and bisexual male-to-female transmission of HIV. In addition, the risk of acquiring syphilis is rising in the homosexual community. Parents of LGBT teens must be aware of the heightened STD risks in this group and actively communicate with their teens about this issue.

Are U.S. Teens More Sexually Active Than Teens in Other Countries?

Teens in the U.S. begin having sex at earlier ages than teens in other developed countries, but once they start having sex, levels of teen sexual activity appear to be similar across major developed countries (Canada, Great Britain, France, Sweden, and the U.S.). In the U.S., teens have sex for the first time at age 17 on average, slightly younger than in Canada (17.5) and France (18). This often surprises U.S. parents who may believe that parents in European countries are cavalier about teen sex, and that some European teens are more sexually active. Not true. *However, while levels of sexual activity are similar, the rates of teen pregnancy, teen births, and teen STDs are drastically higher in the U.S. than in most western European countries.*

What's Love Got to Do with It?

Parents, health care providers, and educators tend to focus on the consequences of teen sex and to minimize, or not even recognize, the powerful force behind "teen love." In general, teens are not engaging in random sex. As a matter of fact, surveys show that 85% of teens feel that sex should occur only in long-term, committed relationships. When teens attending our seminars were asked about the most important factor in determining when they would have sex, "feeling in love," had the top ranking.

In our efforts to prevent early and risky teen sex, we must also appreciate that romantic feelings between teens can be just as strong—or even stronger—than those between adults. Encouraging teens to express their affection in age-appropriate ways is the key. You'll learn more about how to do this in Chapter 5.

Teen Attitudes About Sex: Naiveté, Denial, and Misinformation

You may be startled to learn how your teen thinks about sex, what he or she believes actually constitutes "sex" and what "sexually active" means. Knowing more about what your teen is thinking lets you frame your conversations so you are speaking the same language, even when you want to communicate a vastly different message from what your teen currently understands.

Your definition of "sexually active" may be a far cry from what your teen is thinking. I recently asked one of my teen patients, "Are you sexually active?" Her response was a curious, but very honest, "What exactly do you mean by that?" She went on to ask whether hand touching of her vagina by her partner counted. This encounter reminded me that the words "sexually active" can be unclear. If she had responded yes, I would have assumed that she was having sexual intercourse when this is not what she meant. It's not just parents but also health care providers who need to understand how important it is to communicate clearly when we're talking to teens about sex.

A recent study revealed that some teens don't consider themselves "sexually active" if they had had sex only one or two times. These teens may define "active" as having sex very frequently. In these cases, a teen who claims "I'm not sexually active" can, of course, get pregnant or contract an STD even if sex happens only once or twice.

A few years ago, I attended a party where parents talked about the usual: their kids' schools, teachers, sports, and so on. Then the conversation turned to oral sex. I knew of reports describing oral sex at teen parties as being akin to a modern-day "spin-the-bottle" game, but this was the first time I'd heard any gut reactions from parents. After a few parents got in their "Oh my God!" or, "Can you believe it?" the discussion turned to, "What is up with all of this?"

It's important for parents to know that many teens who engage in oral and even anal sex still consider themselves virgins. One study showed that 59% of all teens and 62% of teen girls did not consider oral sex to be sex. Information collected from the National Survey of Family Growth indicates that a little over 50% of 15- to 19-year-old boys and girls have had oral sex with someone of the opposite sex. Approximately 11% of teens in this age group have had anal sex. Being aware of these statistics will allow you to be better prepared to address concerns about these behaviors with your teen.

I recall one parent's experience, who said she felt "sick to her stomach" when she found out that her daughter had had oral sex. Even more stunning to her than her daughter's behavior was her attitude. She could hardly believe it when her daughter said, "I don't see why you're making such a big deal out of it." Fortunately, this mom had a very open relationship with her daughter and was able to sit her down and point out that oral sex is a very intimate act with emotional consequences, and that she didn't feel it was appropriate behavior for her. Because she was a nurse educator and knowledgeable about the subject, she was also able to communicate about the STD risks associated with oral sex. The good news is that her daughter "got it."

Her daughter's initial "no big deal" reaction reveals an often sharp disconnect between what parents consider to be very intimate sexual behavior, and what teens airily toss off as "not really sex," as if oral or anal intercourse are advanced forms of fooling around, a bit beyond kissing, but not really sex. ***Many teens falsely believe that only vaginal-penile intercourse, where the boy's penis enters the girl's vagina, counts as "sex."***

A very common activity among teens is mutual masturbation. During this activity there is no vaginal, oral, or anal penetration with the penis. Teens stimulate each other's genitals with their hands, with or without clothing on. This activity was once called "heavy petting," but now may be considered just "fooling around" or placed in the catchall category of "hooking up." While mutual masturbation is safer than anal, oral, or vaginal sex, it is not risk-free. STD transmission can occur with this activity.

Combating Teen Naiveté, Denial, and Misinformation

- Be sure your teen understands that oral sex and anal sex are real forms of sex. Both can lead to STDs.

- Inform your teen that "heavy petting" or mutual masturbation aren't 100% risk-free and that some STDs can be transmitted by just "skin-to-skin contact." (You'll find out more about STD transmission in Chapter 4.)

- Understand that words are important. Say what you mean.

  For example, instead of saying, "I believe you should wait to have sex until you're an adult," you will be clearer and more direct if you say, "I believe you should wait until you're an adult to have sexual relationships. That includes oral and anal sex as well as sexual intercourse."

- Keep in mind that a general term like "sexually active" may not be clear enough when you are talking with your teen.

- Be clear about what types of intimate behavior are acceptable to you. Think about where you draw the line and ask yourself, "Am I being realistic?"

- Use brochures/pamphlets and other aids to help your teen explore risk-free ways of showing affection. A great brochure is "101 Ways to Make Love Without Doing It," which is available online at **www.etr.org** (brochure #063).

Where and When Teens Have Sex

Most parents are unaware of where or when their teens usually have sex. Hint: It's not the back seat of a car, as was once the stereotype.

Test your knowledge by answering the following questions:

1. Where are teens most likely to have sex?

    a. Friend's home

    b. Partner's family home

    c. Car or truck

    d. Their own home

2. What percentage of teen females has their first sexual encounter in the teen boy's family home?

    a. 10%

    b. 39%

    c. 50%

3. What time of the day are teens most likely to have sex?

    a. 3–6 p.m.

    b. 6–10 p.m.

    c. 10 p.m.–7 a.m.

4. What month ranks highest for teens having their first sexual encounter?

    a. January

    b. June

    c. August

5. What days of the week are the most common for teens to have sex?

    a. Saturday/Sunday

    b. Sunday/Monday

    c. Friday/Saturday

Answers (1-b, 2-b, 3-b, 4-b, 5-c)

What does this mean? In short, your teen is most likely to have sex in the home of his or her partner on a Friday or Saturday night between the hours of 6 p.m. and 10 p.m. in the month of June. But that's not all. A recent online survey of 10,000 showed that 14% of teens reported having had sex at school.

In school? Parents may ask, "How can this be?" Examples include oral sex at the back of the bus on the way home from a field trip, sex in a corner of the school library, or sex against the hood of a car in the school parking lot.

Reducing Risks Related to Where and When

- Encourage and support weekend and nighttime activities at your teen's school and in your community.
- Realize that there is no substitute for supervision of your teen.
- Set firm curfews and enforce them.
- Prohibit coed slumber parties and check to be sure a responsible adult will be at any party your teen attends.
- Be involved in the PTA or similar organization at your teen's school and voice your concerns about any rumors or reports of sex on school grounds.

Influences on Teen Sexual Behavior

What causes one teen to start having sex at 14 and another teen to wait until she's in college or married to have sex? Let's look at the major influences, and what we, as parents, can do to exert equal or greater impact on our teens' attitudes and behavior.

Television/Media. According to one study, youth spend an average of more than seven hours per day immersed in the media. And, they are receiving a heavy dose of sexual material, including pornography. Research focused on 10- to 17-year-olds and found that *almost half* of the Internet users had viewed pornography in the previous year.

Television shows are significant fodder for sex with 75% of all prime-time shows containing sexual material. And, teen shows on television have more sexual content than shows geared toward adults.

Teens regularly watch sit-coms with references to oral sex, dramas where minors have sex as casually as they make a trip to the mall, and music videos where boys and girls drape suggestively over each other or simulate sex with a pole. The girls in music videos often wear shorts that could double as underwear, skirts that more resemble a belt, and sheer, tight tops stretched over obviously implanted, outsized breasts. The boys waggle their tongues and grab their crotches. Song lyrics taunt teens to "lick it like a lollipop," "put my pussy on it," or "get your dick rubbed." These sounds and images are so commonplace that teens don't bat an eye.

To compound the problem, this type of sexual content on TV, in movies, or on websites often fails to portray the consequences of sexual activity. Information about birth control or safe sex is rarely presented during those steamy sex scenes. Recent statistics reveal that only about 10% of the top shows with sexual material depicted any risks or responsibilities. The point of this discussion is not to protest vulgarity in our culture, but to sharpen your awareness of its implications for your teen. What does all this exposure to sexual content mean?

Research shows that teens who view high levels of television with sexual content were two times more likely to experience teen pregnancy when compared to teens who viewed minimal levels of sexual content. Long-term study results now confirm that heavy exposure to sexual material in mainstream media is associated with earlier sexual intercourse and a greater risk for STDs, as well as unplanned teen pregnancy.

One explanation for this increased risk is that these media depictions of sex promote having sex as normal behavior for teens and as being risk-free.

Managing Media Influences

- Monitor your teens' TV viewing and watch TV as a family whenever possible.

- Discuss your values and reasons for either approving of or disapproving of certain TV shows and movies.

- Have conversations about TV shows/movies that depict sexual encounters, what they mean, and how close they are to reality.

- Talk to your teen about why song lyrics that are demeaning to women, promote casual sex, and contain offensive language are harmful.

- Start your own "booty boycott" and write, call, or e-mail any television or radio station that you believe airs sexually explicit or degrading material to teens.

- Band with other parents to let media outlets know that you won't purchase products advertised or depicted on programs that are objectionable.

- Learn more from the Parents Television Council at **www.parentstv.com.**

Social Networking, Text Messages, E-Mail. Any parent would be delighted to have a son or daughter named "Best Personality" or "Most Likely to Succeed." These yearbook titles we remember from our own school days now have alarming Internet counterparts that would make most parents blush. These include "Most Likely to Have STDs" and "Biggest Slut"—real categories on an actual, anonymous website where students' names are posted. The site receives thousands of "hits" every day. These offensive examples illustrate just one aspect of the alarming sexual landscape that teens now must navigate.

In addition to the Internet, an actual phone call, where one teen speaks "live" to another, is fast going the way of the rotary dial phone. Teens use their cell phones and social networking pages (Facebook, Twitter, among others) to let their friends know where they are, what they're doing, and with whom, complete with pictures and videos that detail their activities. Sexually explicit pages abound, with boys rating girls' bodies complete with sly photos taken with cell phones. With unlimited access to these pages and without any direction from you, teens can become accustomed to the idea that casual sex is not only "no big deal," but no cause for privacy, either.

The mother of a 14-year-old girl somewhat guiltily checked her daughter's cell phone after her daughter left it on the kitchen counter, and was appalled to find text messages from the daughter's 16-year-old boyfriend that contained nude pictures of her ninth-grader. Perhaps some intuition prompted her to stealthily check the phone, but she had no idea her daughter was engaged in this behavior, and was belatedly placed in the position of trying to rein in an out-of-control situation with her very young teen daughter.

Teens sending nude photos via cell phone or "sexting" has become a major concern for parents, with one in five teens admitting they have sent nude or seminude photos of themselves via electronic channels or posted them online. And, these activities have been found to increase the forward or aggressive behavior of many teens.

The casual "sup" (what's up?) in a text message is nothing to worry about, naturally, but you'll want to be alert for more secretive and sexual messages your teen may send or receive. Some teens, especially very young teens, may send sexual messages as a way of trying to appear older, more cool, or more mature. These messages may not always mean that the teens sending and receiving them are actually having sex, but the aggressive suggestions are a risky first step that needs to be curtailed.

Reducing teen pregnancy or encouraging teens to delay having sex isn't a simple matter of turning off the TV, of course, or even of limiting what teens see on television, at the movies, or on the Internet. It's a matter of being aware that teens are bombarded with images of sexual behavior not only on television, but in ads for everything from clothing to makeup to food, in movies, and on websites. There isn't a way to completely shelter your child from these sexual images, but you *can* have ongoing discussions with your teen about what these images portray, how realistic the scenarios are, and whether the people shown match the way your teen wants to be viewed and treated by peers.

Handling Tech-Savvy Teens

- Warn your teens never to send or forward e-mails with nude photos of themselves or their friends, or that contain sexually graphic comments. Tell your teen, sexting is not funny or cool and it is considered a criminal sex offense in some states.

- Talk with your teen about how inappropriate sexual images/comments sent on electronic devices or posted on social networking sites can damage their chances for acceptance into the college of their choice or even limit their future career choices. Colleges and future employers are checking these sites.

- Place parental controls on computers/Blackberrys, etc. to block access to high-risk, graphic material.

- Visit **www.thenationalcampaign.org/sextech** for more detailed information on this subject.

Peer Pressure—Less Potent Than You Think?

Who's a virgin? Who isn't? The halls and classrooms of your teen's middle or high school very likely buzz with an undercurrent of gossip about who belongs in which camp, who is "hooking up" with whom, what they've done and where. Teens naturally want to fit in, be accepted, and have things in common with their peers, so "peer pressure" may seem like the natural place to point the finger when we talk about teens and sex.

However, surveys often don't support the belief that peer pressure is the single most important culprit driving teens toward having sex. In a large national survey done by the National Campaign to Prevent Teen Pregnancy, teens stated that their parents were most influential in the decisions they made about sex, not peers, educators, or others. Among the teens who have attended my seminars on teen pregnancy prevention, only 5% felt that peer pressure was the most important factor in their decisions about sex.

Parents, on the other hand, are more likely than teens to cite friends as the most powerful factor in influencing teen sex—41% in the national survey, and 40% of parents attending my seminars. So who's correct in measuring the impact of peer pressure on teen sexual behavior, parents or teens? That depends on who the friends are, of course, how old they are, and how those friends behave. Let's look at what we know about the dynamics of teen relationships and instances where peers may sway behavior.

Friends' Ages and Attitudes. Studies confirm that teens are more likely to have sex if their friends have more permissive values about sex or are having sex. They are also more likely to have sex if their best friends and peers are older. Teens going steady have a higher chance of becoming sexually active. And if their partner is three or more years older, the odds of them having sex are even higher. The younger the teen, the higher the chance that having an older partner will lead to sexual activity.

Dealing with Peers

While you can't control all the people your teen will come into contact with or whom they will choose as friends, you *can*:

- Insist on meeting your teen's friends.

- Tell your teen if there's something about one of his or her friends that disturbs you (for example, someone who brags about sexual experiences).

- Make every effort to become acquainted with the families of your teen's friends.

- Discourage your teen from "hanging out" with teens who are more than two years older.

Partner vs. Peer Pressure. Surveys from The National Campaign to Prevent Teen Pregnancy show that many young teens feel pressure to have sex. And, many teens 14 and younger say they really didn't want to have sex but they just went along with it. They don't report being forced, but the phrase "just went along with it" doesn't imply an active choice, either. It's important to note that many teens have conflicted feelings about having sex, especially the first time. Two out of three teen girls and over one out of three teen boys report having "mixed feelings" about the first time they had sex.

Dating Guidelines

- Understand that children who feel loved and receive strong nurturing are more likely to have high self-esteem and are better able to resist peer pressure to have sex.

- Communicate to your teen that a boyfriend/girlfriend who really cares about them will never pressure them to have sex.

- Set guidelines for dating, including the following:

    o   Beginning dating—Suggest group dating for 13- to 15-year-olds.

    o   Strongly discourage single dating before your teen reaches age 16.

    o   Be wary of your teen dating someone three or more years older.

- Set clear curfews—this can vary according to age, but for age 16 consider no later than 12 p.m.

Alcohol, Drugs, and Teen Sex

Add alcohol and/or drugs to the already combustible mix of teens, hormones, and peer pressure, and all bets are off. Even teens who may not want to have sex yet may find themselves in out-of-control situations if they or a partner has been drinking alcohol, smoking pot, or using other drugs. Many studies correlate teen alcohol and illegal drug use with teens having sex, having sex more frequently, and having more partners than teens who do not use alcohol or drugs.

According to a recent National Youth Risk Behavior Surveillance survey, slightly more than two in 10 kids said they drank alcohol or used drugs prior to their last sexual encounter. Not only high school teens are vulnerable to the risk of alcohol, drugs, and sex. A study of multicultural college women at a Southern California university showed that a majority of these older teens place themselves at risk by using alcohol and drugs and participating in sexual activity. The study found that "despite knowing the risk," 52% of these teen women used drugs and alcohol during sex.

Helping Teens Avoid Alcohol and Drugs

- Reinforce warnings about the dangers of alcohol and drug use, and reiterate that underage drinking and all drug use is illegal.

- Let your teen know that teen girls are more likely to have unprotected sex and become pregnant or acquire an STD when they've been drinking alcohol or using drugs.

- Check to see if your child's school offers the DARE program or another drug/alcohol prevention and education program. If not, consult with your local police department to find a program near you.

- Verify that parents you can trust are present at any party your child attends. Don't be afraid to call and speak with the parents yourself.

TEENS, SEX, AND VIOLENCE

Along with helping your teen to avoid early sex, pregnancy, and STDs, another essential aspect of your role as a parent is shielding your child from sexual assault. We've heard the sensational cases of alleged or confirmed sexual assault in prominent families, at Ivy League colleges, and elite military academies. Sexual assault in the teen population cuts across ethnic, racial, socioeconomic, and cultural boundaries, leaving victims with painful and lasting scars.

Adolescent Dating Violence

The term "adolescent dating violence" (ADV, also known as teen dating violence) describes physical, emotional, or sexual violence within an adolescent partner relationship. Girls are much more likely to be victims although ADV affects boys too. Gay, lesbian, and bisexual youth are also at risk. In our electronic age, teens may also experience digital abuse. Examples include being harassed by a partner through cell phones and texting or being the victim of an online post meant to humiliate or embarrass them. Teen victims of ADV are at increased risk for depression, anxiety, poor self-esteem, alcohol and drug abuse, eating disorders, sexual health risks, and pregnancy.

Date Rape

One in four U.S. college students surveyed reports having experienced an attempted or complete rape. And 9% of high school students report having been "forced" to have sex.

Many sexual assaults occur in young people who are under the influence of drugs or alcohol. Alcohol is commonly associated with date rape and, alarmingly, in the majority of cases the substance abuse was voluntary, not forced.

Many parents have heard the term "date rape drug." I have had young women as patients whose histories strongly suggested they had been victims of date rape drugs. These illegal drugs, easily acquired on the Internet, are colorless, odorless, and tasteless, and can be slipped into a drink. Date rape drugs are not detectable in standard drug testing done in the emergency room.

In the young patients I've seen where I've suspected date rape, their stories were difficult to piece together. Date rape drugs leave their victims unable to remember anything about the assault. It is not uncommon for victims of date rape drugs to seek medical attention several days after being raped.

That was true in Melody's case, a young woman in her late teens who came to the emergency room reporting that she thought she had been raped. She recalled being at a party several days earlier, and leaving the party with a group of people. After that there was a sizeable gap in her memory, until she woke up not knowing where she was or whom she had been with. She was naked from the waist down. Melody said she was "too embarrassed" to report the incident to the police, but several days later she came to the ER for help with the anxiety and fear she was experiencing.

Protecting Teens Against Dating Violence/Rape

- Tell your teen—in no uncertain terms—that abuse, in any form, is never acceptable behavior.

- Remind your teen that alcohol and/or drug use can impair judgment and lead to poor choices and risky behavior.

- Petition your teen's middle or high school to promote awareness of adolescent dating violence and the powerful risks associated with drinking, date rape drugs, and sexual assault.

- Go to **futureswithoutviolence.org** to learn more about adolescent dating violence education.

Other Influences on Teen Sex

There are many social risk factors associated with early and/or risky teen sex. Teens who live in communities with higher levels of poverty and violence, or who grow up in homes where there is physical abuse are at increased risk for early sexual activity. Gang involvement has also been shown to raise the risk. Teens in single parent homes or whose mothers were teen parents themselves are also at greater risk for early sexual involvement. And, teens whose older brothers or sisters had early sex are more likely to repeat the behavior.

Academic factors associated with early sex behavior include poor academic achievement, lower academic expectations—e.g., not being expected to go to college, and lower levels of educational attainment by the teen's parents.

There are also significant racial differences regarding teen sex behavior. According to the most recent findings from the Youth Risk Behavior Surveillance, black teens are most likely to report ever having sex, followed by Hispanic and then white teens.

Overcoming Challenging Social Issues

- Seek support from family members and friends to help guide your teen—especially important for single parents.

- Involve your child in extracurricular activities like scouting and sports.

- Seek out the community resources such as the YMCA, Big Brothers/Big Sisters, or 4-H Clubs—especially important if you live in a disadvantaged community (contact information in Chapter 10).

- Be knowledgeable about your child's academic progress. If your teen is underachieving, understand that your child may be at higher risk for early sexual activity and intervene early. Meet with his/her teachers to discuss ways to help your child. Seek out tutors/mentors.

Decreasing Your Teen's Risk

The following section will review characteristics that have been shown to *decrease the risk* that your teen will engage in early, risky sexual behavior.

Family Dynamics. A strong family provides a powerful means of guiding, instructing, and disciplining teens, creating an environment where they can develop into independent, thriving, loving adults. These family characteristics are known to help reduce the likelihood of teens having sex early:

- Teens' strong emotional attachments to their parents and higher levels of feeling connected and satisfied with their relationships

- Presence of two parents in the home

- Higher levels of parental educational attainment (i.e., having completed more education)

- Greater parental supervision and monitoring

- Greater parental disapproval of premarital/teen sex

- Greater parental communication with their teen about sex

Positive Peer Influences. While it's easy to get lost in worry about the influences we wish we could shield our children from, it's important to remember that peers can constructively influence our teens, too, with acceptance, listening, and feedback, and by acting as positive role models. Think about this: according to the National Survey of Family Growth, the majority of teens disapprove of other teens 16 and younger having sex. Surprising, but it's a fact you can take advantage of. And remember, knowing your teen's friends and their parents helps you to encourage those relationships that support your values and expectations.

Religious/Spiritual Training. For many teens, their religious or spiritual background is a powerful source of guidance or an inner voice that helps to shape their thinking about sexual behavior. According to the National Campaign to Prevent Teen Pregnancy, the primary reason teens cited for not having sex was that it was "against religion or morals."

Teens with greater religious involvement (worship attendance, perceived importance of religion, and frequency of praying) were shown to have lower-risk sexual behavior. In contrast, teens in ninth to 12th grades with less religious involvement were more likely to participate in riskier sexual behavior.

Parents can include their religious beliefs and perspectives on faith in their conversations with their teens about sex. This can help to positively influence their behavior.

Participation in Sports. Research has shown that girls who participated in sports were more likely to remain virgins and more likely to begin sex later in adolescence than their peers who weren't involved in sports. The study also found that girls active in sports were likely to have fewer partners after they began having sex.

Girls who participate in sports have the benefit of frequent interaction with a responsible, caring adult. And another benefit of girls playing sports is that it takes their focus off dating and boys. Continuing to support sports programs for girls, both school- and community-based, is an important avenue for helping to decrease early sexual activity among teen girls.

Volunteerism. Teens who participate in extracurricular activities by either volunteering in their communities or by being involved in community-sponsored activities are at lower risk for sexual activity and pregnancy. Educators and health officials agree that teens who are involved in community service gain many advantages, among them self-respect.

School Achievement. Teens who feel connected to their school, who are highly motivated, and who actively participate in the academic process are less likely to have sex at an early age. Similarly, teens who receive good grades and those who attend schools with low rates of absenteeism are also more likely to postpone having sex.

Sex Education. Chapter 6 discusses the role of school-based sex education in delaying teen sexual activity and preventing pregnancy and STDs.

Knowledgeable Parents Are Powerful Parents

If you read this chapter with your eyes partially covered with one hand, reluctant to peer beyond the last paragraph for fear of what you might find—congratulations, you made it through! You can now consider yourself a well-informed parent on the issues of teen sexual attitudes and behavior. Yes, you have appropriate concerns, but now you have less need to worry about "Teens Gone Wild." You're ready to go forward, to continue learning, and to become an even more empowered parent.

Chapter 3

Teen Pregnancy: Changed Lives, Untold Consequences

If our American way of life fails the child, it fails us all.

—Pearl S. Buck

My desire to do something to help reduce the sobering rates of teen pregnancy in our country propelled me to take on the role of chair of my hospital's Teen Pregnancy and STD Prevention Program in 1997. What I've learned since beginning that journey has been tremendous—profound, disturbing, and compelling. In this chapter, I will share information that will help you understand the problem of teen pregnancy, and what it really means for teens, their families, and our society.

Enduring Stories

I still remember my first encounter with teen pregnancy. I was about 13 when I learned that Trina, a 15-year-old girl who attended our combined middle school and high school, was pregnant. This occurred four decades ago in a small Midwestern community. At that time, this type of news was shocking to students and parents, and word spread very quickly.

What I remember most is how Trina, a beautiful, dark-haired girl and former cheerleader, seemed so all alone in the world. She had her family, but I sensed that she carried the weight of the world on her shoulders, painfully aware of every pointed glance and hearing every whispered comment from schoolmates as her belly grew. There was no special school for pregnant teens to attend, so Trina continued to attend our public school until her baby was born. However, her education was interrupted for months as she neared the end of her pregnancy. Perhaps more importantly, her life was irrevocably altered.

- Extracurricular activities, including cheerleading, were out.

- Normal teenage experiences like school dances, shopping with friends, and just "hanging out" ceased to exist.

- Relationships with family members were affected as parents and siblings helped to absorb additional responsibilities, as well as added stress.

The early insight I gained from observing Trina's situation was that unintended teenage pregnancy had a significant impact on everyone involved, and that after such an event just about everything in that young person's life would change. The way pregnant teens are viewed and accepted has evolved, but the difficulties that arise in their lives and in the lives of their loved ones remain unaltered.

Consider the comments from Linda, a teen parent who wrote to "Dear Abby" a few years ago:

> "I was not, and still am not, emotionally prepared to be a mother. The stress is incredible. For the rest of my life I am going to be a mother. There is no way around it. If I don't feel like being a mother at some point in time and want to just go out and be an 18-year-old typical teenager having fun—that's too bad, because I will always be a mother first."

She went on, "Thank you, Abby. I hope I have prevented one teenage pregnancy with this letter." Linda's story illustrates how an unintended teen pregnancy and early motherhood are so often associated with a heaviness about the responsibilities, instead of the overwhelming joy more mature women experience when their pregnancies are intended.

As an obstetrician, I have also witnessed, up close and personal, the emotional devastation felt by parents when they learn their teen daughter is pregnant. One of the most gut-wrenching examples in my practice involved a 15-year-old, Kim, who came in for her first appointment when she was five months pregnant. Her mother, Janet, was with her, and I can still remember the shock on her face when she learned Kim was pregnant. Janet expressed that she held a deep religious belief and that the thought of abortion would have been unimaginable before this. But the stress of the situation caused Kim's mother, who was obviously unnerved, to suddenly blurt, "If she wasn't so far along, I'd actually want her to have an abortion—I can't believe this has happened!"

Janet is not the first parent I have witnessed, nor will she likely be the last, whose outlook and values dramatically change when confronted with the reality of a teen pregnancy.

Another very difficult situation I recall vividly involved Cindy, another 15-year-old. Cindy came to my office with her grandmother. She seemed anxious and reported that she had missed several periods. Cindy's pregnancy test was positive and the ultrasound I performed showed a normally developing 6-month fetus. Ordinarily I love the days when, as a doctor and a mother myself, I have the privilege of breaking joyous news of a pregnancy to a now-expecting woman and her family, but this was decidedly not one of those days.

Cindy's grandmother broke down in tears after learning the news. Her tears, combined with the somber way she held her head in her hands, conveyed a keen sense of grief and despair. She appeared to be dazed and in shock as she asked, "How could this have happened?" In seconds, her vision of what her granddaughter's life would have been like had vanished.

I have also been struck by heart-wrenching reactions from parents outside the office setting as well. One of my friends, who raised her granddaughter, Debra, shared the feelings she experienced after learning that Debra was pregnant at age 17. She said with an almost palpable heaviness,

"I feel sadness that Debra had to grow up so fast. When she told me she thought she was pregnant, I was in shock and disbelief. I thought Debra had been on birth control, had her head on straight, and was too smart to let this happen. I was also angry, frustrated and, quite frankly, worried about the impact on my life. I also felt that she had no clue about what this would mean to her life and how quickly everything was about to change."

This grandmother's sentiments are very real, although many adults may not acknowledge their secret worry or even resentment that a teen pregnancy in the family throws their lives into chaos, too.

Debra's grandmother continued, "Today, Debra's life is very different from her friends' lives, most of whom are away at college. Instead of experiencing her 20s like her friends, she has taken on a tremendous responsibility for another human being, while she is still developing herself."

Over and over again, we are reminded that the first news of an unintended teen pregnancy is still met with shock, heartache, and a looming sense of despair by the parents. Whether the teen pregnancy occurs in a celebrity household or in a less visible, more ordinary family, the reactions are strikingly similar. These parents, soon to be grandparents, know all too well of the struggles involved in raising kids when the moms and dads are emotionally mature, financially secure, and have at least a high school education. The gigantic hurdles faced by teens who are not emotionally equipped to be parents, financially dependent on their own parents, and still in high school or middle school, can seem overwhelming.

In the sections that follow, we'll explore the ramifications of teen pregnancy for the individual, family, and community. We'll review the serious social and health consequences of teen pregnancy, important facts about the face of teen pregnancy today, and the major risk factors for becoming a pregnant teen.

The All-Too-Real Impact of Teen Pregnancy

The majority of Americans acknowledge that teen pregnancy is a huge problem in our country, but how many truly understand just what those consequences are? Teen pregnancy can have an enormously negative impact on individuals, families, communities, and the nation. As one young teen starkly put it, "Teen pregnancy can ruin your life."

While the obstacles associated with unintended teen pregnancy can be overcome, the hurdles can never be taken lightly. Let's take a closer look at the specific consequences of teen pregnancy.

- *Teens who become pregnant face major educational disadvantages.*

Teen mothers who give birth before age 18 are significantly less likely to graduate from high school. The ramifications of this are disheartening. In our fast-paced, technologically savvy world, an abbreviated education places teen moms at a huge disadvantage in competing for good jobs, decent wages, and optimal living conditions.

If the teen mother completes high school, she's much less likely than her counterparts to go to college. In fact, only 2% of teens who give birth before age 18 earn a college degree by age 30.

A pregnant teen often doesn't fully comprehend the impact of an abbreviated education until later in life. I think of Sharon, now 25 and a mother of two. She had her first daughter at age 16. Although she did obtain her General Educational Development (GED) diploma eventually, she laments the fact that her dream of becoming an architect is very unlikely to become a reality. There's no way she can envision having the time or money to go back to school. She finds herself completely stretched to the limits taking care of her kids and working at a relatively low-paying job. And, she's one of the lucky ones because she married her baby's father and they remain together after eight years.

While it is beyond the scope of this book to address how pregnant moms can be helped to achieve the minimum of a basic high school education, I want to remind parents that preventing teen pregnancy is critical in order to avoid undermining the education of so many teen girls. John F. Kennedy summed up the importance of education very eloquently when he said:

> "Let us think of education as the means of developing our greatest abilities, because in each of us there is a private hope and dream which, fulfilled, can be translated into benefit for everyone and greater strength for our nation."

A teen girl with an unintended pregnancy does potentially forfeit her private dreams for the future, and places at risk her opportunity to contribute to a larger, public good.

- *Pregnant teens are at increased risk for poverty.*

This should come as no surprise after learning about the likelihood that a pregnant teen's formal education is not only interrupted, but often completely halted. Think about the following statistic:

According to The National Campaign to Prevent Teen Pregnancy, **teen mothers are much more likely to receive welfare within a few years after the birth of their first child.** The combination of youth, limited education, and largely unmarried status all contribute to the combustible combination that makes poverty a near certainty for teen moms. And teen fathers don't fare much better since they are much less likely to complete high school, earn a college degree, or obtain a higher paying job when compared with teen men who don't become teen dads. It's critical to keep in mind that the higher rates of poverty for teen moms and dads translate into higher rates of poverty for their children.

And while economic disadvantage is a powerful adverse consequence for teen parents, the ripple effect on society is astounding. It's been reported that the national costs for teen pregnancy to taxpayers is several billion dollars per year. The costs include welfare payments, public health services, lost taxes, support services for their children, and more. In fact, over seven in 10 teen births in this country are covered by Medicaid. As we'll review later in this chapter, the high risk of poverty is not only a consequence of teen pregnancy, but a risk factor as well.

• *The children of teen parents are at increased medical, educational, and social risk.*

Babies born to teen moms have a higher chance of being born premature, with one study reporting a 65% higher risk of being delivered before 32 weeks (eight weeks before the due date). Associated with premature birth, these babies of teen moms have an increased risk of being underweight at delivery (low birth weight). Both premature birth and low birth weight place these babies at higher risk of medical complications including blindness, deafness, lung disease, bleeding in the brain, and more.

You've seen images of tiny, premature babies in high-level nurseries with multiple tubes protruding from their bodies and breathing tubes hooked to gigantic respiratory machines. The fragile and delicate beginnings that these babies face are difficult enough. Add to this the challenge of being raised by a teen mom, often with no involvement by the baby's father, and the hard road ahead becomes painfully clear.

Children born to unmarried teen mothers who have not completed high school are significantly more likely to live in poverty than the children of their married, adult counterparts who graduated from high school. The sons of teen mothers are more likely to end up in prison than the sons of mothers who delay childbearing to at least age 20.

In addition, babies born to teen moms are more likely to suffer from mental retardation, learning difficulties, and emotional disorders like anxiety and low self-esteem.

• *Teen moms are at higher risk for other health issues.*

Teen moms have been found to be more likely to smoke cigarettes during their pregnancies. Tobacco use has been shown to increase the likelihood of preterm labor and low-birth-weight babies.

Teen moms are also much more likely than older moms to register later for care in their pregnancies. It's not unusual for a teen to see a doctor for the first time when she's almost halfway through her pregnancy, as the stories about Kim and Cindy point out. When this occurs, her health care provider misses an opportunity to perform important prenatal tests early. For example, when an ultrasound is done later in the pregnancy, it's not as accurate in confirming the due date. Or, when a blood test that checks for anemia is delayed, treatment for iron deficiency is delayed and this can affect the baby's growth. These teens are also late in receiving healthy information about their diets and self-care during the pregnancy. And significant problems like diabetes, which can adversely impact the pregnancy, are addressed much later than they should be.

Some studies have found that rates of depression are higher in pregnant teens than in older pregnant women. One study found that over one in five pregnant teens was reported to be depressed during her pregnancy. This factor may explain some of the reports of teen moms who leave their newborn babies in trash cans or harm them in other ways. Many of you may remember the 1996 story of Amy Grossberg and Brian Peterson. This teen couple somehow kept her pregnancy secret from their family, friends, and teachers. They went to a motel when it was time to give birth and then killed their baby boy. Amy was quoted as saying she wanted the pregnancy to "go away."

Finally, I want to address some serious health concerns that may occur closer to the time of delivery or during labor. Teens may experience a potentially serious medical condition in pregnancy known as pregnancy-induced hypertension or pre-eclampsia. In this condition, the teen's blood pressure rises, sometimes markedly, and this may adversely affect her kidney, liver, and brain. In worst-case scenarios, seizures, stroke, and even death can occur. I have witnessed several cases of severe pre-eclampsia in teens. We all want to think of childbirth as a joyous experience where family members anxiously await the newborn with colorful balloons and delicious-smelling flowers. The last thing families want to consider is the mom experiencing a frightening seizure, followed by monitoring in an intensive care unit.

I also want to mention that other very serious complications can occur during childbirth. Like pre-eclampsia, these are not limited to teens by any means, but when they occur in very young girls who never intended to be pregnant in the first place, the human toll seems even more magnified. I will always remember Leiana, who at 16 was rushed to the hospital because of bleeding. She ended up with an emergency cesarean section because her placenta had separated from the wall of her uterus. Unfortunately, her baby boy didn't survive, which was a crushing blow to Leiana. The fact that her pregnancy was unintended did not diminish her heartache. Then, there was 15-year-old Sharon, who bled so profusely after her delivery that she needed a transfusion of several units of blood and then had to be cared for in the intensive care unit for several days. Sharon's little girl did well, but the jarring memories of this experience will undoubtedly stay with this young mother forever.

- *Teen pregnancy is associated with a myriad of social issues.*

Perhaps the most significant social factor aside from age influencing the outcome of teen childbearing is the reality that the vast majority of teen pregnancies occur in unmarried girls. Greater than *eight in 10 teen births occur in unmarried teens* and this number has increased from *1.5 in 10 births* among unmarried teens in 1960. While out-of-wedlock births have increased in all age groups, many adverse effects of single parenthood are more pronounced in undereducated, less mature, and financially unprepared teen moms.

Most pregnant teen girls do not marry the biological fathers of their babies. Even when pregnant teens do marry the father of their babies, the marriages are two to three times more likely to end in divorce than people who marry in their 20s. I'm not citing this statistic to suggest that marriage between parents guarantees happiness or success. However, single teens face more hardships in raising their children and the absence of a loving, supportive partner only adds to the difficulty.

It is true that in some cultures, teen marriage by age 18 or 19 is more common and, in some cases, support for pregnancy in this age group is strong. I have cared for several young couples where the pregnant mom was 18 or 19 and either married to or strongly supported by the father of the baby and his family. Because these teens have completed high school and are more mature, their lives may be less disrupted and they and their children often fare better than those unmarried moms younger than 18 at the time they give birth.

There are troubling correlations between teen pregnancy and violence against women as well. According to The National Campaign to Prevent Teen Pregnancy, pregnancy is four to six times higher among high school girls who reported that they had experienced dating violence when compared to their peers who had not experienced such violence. And, pregnant teens report experiencing higher levels of physical abuse at the hands of their partners compared with pregnant women who are older. In these cases, what may have initially begun as a strong emotional attraction can lead not only to an unintended pregnancy, but physical abuse as well.

Another more subtle form of violence against women and teen women especially is the concept of "reproductive coercion." In this situation, boys not only want their girlfriends to get pregnant but are preventing them from using birth control. Just imagine, teen girls becoming pregnant because of inadequate information, carelessness, the lack of access to health care, but also because of coercion at the hands of their partner. This and other forms of sexual violence against women are being addressed by various organizations, including Futures Without Violence.

The bottom line is that teen pregnancy dramatically affects the teen mom, her child, her family, and her community. As we have seen, the all-too-real impact of teen pregnancy is felt in a myriad of areas— education, physical and mental health, socioeconomic well-being, and family dynamics.

The story of Melanie Knight encompasses so many of these issues. Melanie found herself pregnant at age 17. She states that her high school administrators told her that if she hadn't been so close to graduation, they would have advised her to drop out. Melanie's baby was born premature and weighed only 2 pounds, 2 ounces at birth. He required intensive, high-level nursery care for three months. Melanie recounts that this situation was "agonizing."

While Melanie did marry the father of her baby, like so many teen parents they ultimately divorced. To make things worse, the relationship became physically abusive before it ended. As noted previously, teen relationships are at higher risk for becoming physically abusive.

In other ways, Melanie's story took a different path from that of so many unwed teen moms. With the help of her family, she was able to struggle through the difficulties and subsequently attend college. She's now successful and devotes much of her time to working with local high school guidance counselors on the issue of teen pregnancy.

Noteworthy Facts About Teen Pregnancy

- The U.S. has higher teen pregnancy rates than many other comparable industrialized countries.

- Approximately one in four girls in the U.S. gets pregnant before age 20

- The majority of teen pregnancies occur in white, Hispanic and African-American teens.

- Hispanic and African-American teens are dispropor-tionately *affected by teen* pregnancy.

Regarding Teen Birth

- Birth rates for teens in the U.S. are significantly higher than in other similar industrialized countries, like Japan and the Netherlands

- The majority of teen births occur to white teens, followed by Hispanic and then African-American teens.

- Hispanic and African-American teens are *dispropor-tionately affected* by teen birth.

- Approximately fifty-seven percent of teens continue their pregnancies and give birth, twenty-nine percent abort their pregnancies, and fourteen percent experience miscarriage.

These figures serve to demonstrate just how much work needs to be done in the arena of teen pregnancy prevention. The good news is that while teen pregnancy and birth rates in the U.S. have fluctuated over the years, the trend has been downward with significant reductions in the past few years. And while governmental agencies, national organizations, educators, and health professionals all have a very important role to play, we, our teens' parents, who nurture them from birth, have the largest role and the greatest opportunity to make a positive difference.

What Are Major Factors Associated with Teen Pregnancy?

In 2008, many U.S. parents were shaken by the news from one small Massachusetts town called Gloucester. Seventeen girls in one high school became pregnant, which was a fourfold increase compared with 2007. The uproar was compounded by reports of a "pact" reportedly made by the girls to get pregnant and raise their babies together. The story made headlines in all major news outlets.

What was behind this explosion of teen pregnancies in Gloucester? Some theories included:

- A marked reduction in jobs in the community, causing a socioeconomic shift

- An increase in broken families

- Lack of access to women's health care and birth control by teens

- The teen girls' desire for someone who would love them unconditionally

This bombshell story highlights some of the risk factors associated with teen pregnancy in general—socioeconomic disadvantage, lack of access to adequate health care, family dysfunction, and teen attitudes. In the following section, we'll take a look at some of these major factors associated with teen pregnancy.

It's important to bear in mind that a risk factor is just that—one of many possible factors that may be associated with a certain outcome. Many teens who become pregnant have none of the risk factors that we'll discuss. However, in searching for ways to help decrease teen pregnancy, addressing these risks offers an important place to focus our efforts—as parents, health care providers, educators, policymakers, and concerned citizens.

Socioeconomic Disadvantage

Does coming from a financially disadvantaged family and/or community increase the odds that a teen girl will become pregnant or that a teen boy will father a child? What we know is that teens raised in economically disadvantaged families are more likely to start having sex at a younger age and are less likely to use birth control. In turn, these teens are more likely to experience higher rates of pregnancy and childbearing.

We have learned that pregnancy rates are much higher in the U.S. than in most western European countries. However, when we compare the rates of teen pregnancy in eastern European countries like Romania or Bulgaria, where there is greater economic disadvantage, vs. France or the Netherlands, we see much higher rates of teen pregnancy in the former countries. This serves to highlight the role of socioeconomic disadvantage in teen pregnancy risk.

While it is helpful to be aware that socioeconomic status does play a role in teen pregnancy risk, its role in the big picture is not entirely clear. Some studies have actually shown mixed results regarding family income and teen pregnancy risks. Some have concluded that other factors within the family or related to individual characteristics may carry greater weight than family income.

Family Dynamics

You don't choose your family. They are God's gift to you, as you are to them.

—Desmond Tutu

In strong families, children are more likely to grow up with what they need to navigate this complicated and sometimes harsh world. When the family unit is struggling or hurting, children may be less likely to acquire the important tools they need to achieve their highest potential, and this can include learning how to make responsible and healthy choices regarding their sexual health.

Families have many issues to contend with in our fast-paced and ever-changing society. Understanding and identifying the factors within the family that may contribute to a higher likelihood of teen pregnancy is critical for every parent. Knowledge of these factors allows parents an opportunity to address them and, where possible, to take measures to reduce their impact.

Here are some family characteristics that increase the likelihood of early teen sex and pregnancy:

- Lack of communication with teens about sexual health and risk taking

- Permissive attitudes about premarital and/or teen sex

- Early sex and teen pregnancy in older siblings

- Teenage parenthood in the teen's parents—one study showed that 25% of girls born to teen mothers become teen moms themselves

- Abuse of alcohol or illegal drugs by the teen's parents

- Divorce/separation of the teen's parents

Race, Geography, and Culture

As noted, the U.S. leads other similarly developed countries in the rates of teen pregnancy and birth. And Hispanic, African-American, and American Indian teens have disproportionately higher rates of teen pregnancy and birth. However, when education, income, and employment statistics in these communities are taken into consideration, race becomes less important.

When considering race, teen pregnancy, and teen birth—keep in mind that race is just one of many interrelated factors influencing teen pregnancy. And, it is critical for all concerned about this issue to remember that teen pregnancy cuts deeply across all racial boundaries.

Teens living in rural areas have higher teen birth rates compared to those living in urban areas. Differences in access to health care, economics, poverty, and culture are among the factors that play a role.

Over the years, there has been increased acceptance in the U.S. of sex outside of marriage and out-of-wedlock births, which transcends age. The highly sexualized media in our culture has certainly contributed to the changes in attitudes about sex among teens, as noted in Chapter 2. But surely it has also affected the views of others in society as well. Cultural changes, for better or worse, are with us to stay and will continue to evolve over time. Parents must remain vigilant in supervising and guiding their teens regarding sexual messages in all the various media forms and in music, as pointed out in Chapter 2.

Teen Dynamics

The majority of teens who become pregnant do so unintentionally. The portrayal of teen girls wanting to become pregnant just so they can have "someone to love or be loved by" does not appear to be the overwhelming impetus leading to teen pregnancy although it may be a factor in some cases. According to the National Longitudinal Study of Adolescent Health, 16% of teens reported that "getting pregnant at this time would not be so bad." And, another study found that almost 33%

of teen girls who saw a health care professional for pregnancy testing were either disappointed or ambivalent about their negative results.

The really obvious reasons why so many teens become pregnant—having sex and not using birth control, possibly because they didn't have access to it, or using it incorrectly—are easy to understand. However, there are more subtle teen factors that contribute to high rates of teen pregnancy, some of which were highlighted in Chapter 2.

- Peers

  Although peer pressure doesn't seem to be as strong a factor as many parents perceive, the desire to fit in and conform is still especially strong in preteens and younger teens. And, surveys indicate that at least one in three boys and one in four girls ages 15 to 17 report feeling pressure to have sex.

- Romantic feelings

  As noted previously, in surveys done during my tenure as chairperson of our Teen Pregnancy and STD Prevention Program, the majority of teens ranked feeling "in love" as the most important factor in determining when they would have sex. This outranked their parents' influence, peer pressure, and religious beliefs. In all the news reports, magazine accounts, and TV shows alarming parents with every new statistic regarding teen pregnancy, very seldom is this basic, but very potent issue discussed. Intense emotional feelings of love between teens are real and should not be overlooked in our approach to preventing teen pregnancy.

- Changing social norms about sexual behavior and teen pregnancy

  While young males may be expected to "sow their wild oats," there was a time when teen high school girls who had sex were called "bad," "fast," or "slutty." No more. In addition, the social stigma regarding teen pregnancy that led pregnant girls to disappear for several months, secretly have their babies, and place them for adoption before returning to their communities appears to have vanished. Pregnant teens are now very much out in the open.

- Earlier maturation of teens

Studies show that today's teens mature physically at earlier ages. Girls who are physically mature and start having their periods early and appear older than their age are at risk for having sex at an earlier age. Notably, African-American and Hispanic children enter puberty, the medical term for the time of life when a child develops into an adult, earlier than white children. In fact, several studies have shown that African-American females begin the course of their sexual maturation approximately one year earlier than European-American girls. What significance this may have, if any, on the higher rates of teen pregnancy in African-American and Hispanic girls may certainly deserve future study.

The bottom line here is that it can be very challenging for teens who may look like adults physically, but don't have an adult's emotional maturity. Looking like a grown-up and handling grown-up behaviors are two very different things.

- Lack of adequate access to sexual health care

Teens are dependent on everyone around them—parents, educators, health care providers, health care insurers, policymakers—when it comes to having the ability to seek sexual health care and to obtain birth control if they choose to have sex. I'll discuss this very important issue in detail in Chapter 7.

Effects of Alcohol and Drug Use

Parents worry about their kids drinking and driving, and the horrible possibility of a deadly crash. Or they may be nervous about their kids getting hooked on drugs which can thrust their lives into a downward spiral. They must also confront the potential that underage drinking and illicit drug use will lead to teen pregnancy because teens under the influence of alcohol or drugs are more likely to engage in risky sexual behaviors, and act in ways that they wouldn't have had they been sober. Sex and alcohol and/or drugs creates higher odds for unprotected sex, as detailed in Chapter 2.

Looking Past the Pain

Stories about teen pregnancy often, as we have seen at the beginning of this chapter—and justifiably—emphasize the negative consequences. With few exceptions, the initial reaction to an unintended teen pregnancy includes the teen's overwhelming fear, anxiety, and sadness, and the parents' shock, disappointment, anger, and a sense of "what did I/we do wrong?" It's as if almost everyone closely affected by teen pregnancy goes through a grieving process. There's the loss of freedom, a need to grow up too fast, and a seemingly irrevocable alteration in the teen's potential and future. For parents, there is the loss of a certain ideal they may have had for their child, perhaps a sense of shame, and the knowledge that their lives have also been changed forever.

The point I want to make here is that grief often initiates a path toward growth, as well as an opportunity to learn. While it is beyond the scope of this book to expand upon the many issues facing the pregnant teen after she delivers, I do want to acknowledge that this is also a very important issue and that many resources are available on this topic.

What Can Parents Do to Decrease the Risk of Teen Pregnancy?

In this chapter, we've come to understand the important reasons why teen pregnancy is and should be regarded as a major public health problem in our country. The negative consequences range from thwarting a basic education, to increased risks for poverty and lower-paying jobs, to a host of psychosocial and health ills, especially for teen girls. Sadly, the result is often a lower likelihood that an affected teen will achieve her or his fullest potential.

We've also looked at the intolerable statistics which point out that U.S. teens are at much higher risk for teen pregnancy and its associated consequences than teens from other similarly developed countries. This troubling fact will remain a source of national peril until concerned people of all ages and from all walks of life insist on vigilance toward and absolute support of measures known to reduce the risk for all our teens.

As to what parents can do to decrease the risk of teen pregnancy, the answers to this question will continue be explored throughout *Before It's Too Late*. Simple answers? No. Can parents do it alone? No. Are there many resources to assist parents? Yes.

The obvious solution is that anything that parents, educators, health professionals, policymakers, and other concerned adults can do to encourage teens to avoid or delay teen sex and to use reliable birth control consistently if they do choose to have sex is critical.

In looking at the risk factors for teen pregnancy covered in this chapter, there are some circumstances that parents can change and others that are unalterable.

- Parents may not be able to easily improve their socioeconomic status or that of their community, and they may be limited in their ability to change certain family characteristics associated with higher risks of teen pregnancy. They can, however, become more aware of how these dynamics can heighten their teen's risk and take steps to reduce the risk. Many of these steps are outlined in Chapter 2 (increased parental supervision, involving their teens in organizations like YMCA, Big Sister and Big Brother Programs, sports, and after-school activities, etc.).

• Recognizing that racial risks for teen pregnancy disproportionately affect African-American and Hispanic teens can motivate affected parents to be more vigilant in exercising all the strategies outlined in this book to help their teens postpone sex and to use appropriate birth control if they do have sex.

And, we must all acknowledge the cultural shifts that have transformed our society and take measures to lessen factors like the overabundance of sexual images in the media.

• Parents can help their teens to combat peer pressure and to seek age-appropriate ways of expressing affection as discussed in Chapter 2. And parents must remain watchful regarding the risks of alcohol and drugs for their teens and communicate these risks clearly and frequently.

In the chapters that follow, you will be challenged to more clearly assess your own values and to gain greater insight into the complex topic of teen abstinence. You'll find helpful hints on how to talk to and better guide your kids about their sexual health. And, you will be presented with a comprehensive review of birth control, as it relates to teens. The in-depth review of these topics has one goal—decreasing the risk of teen pregnancy in your family and in all our families and communities.

Chapter 4

Sexually Transmitted Diseases: What Parents and Teens May Not Know

They certainly give very strange names to diseases.

—Plato

If parents were told that millions of teens would be injured in automobile accidents each year, would they react with alarm and outrage? Would they rally to insist that their elected representatives and community leaders work to reverse this statistic? No doubt that there would be a deafening outcry.

The bitter truth parents, is that millions of our teens are being injured each year. The injuries aren't due to automobile accidents, but something much more discreet. The culprit is an epidemic of STDs. The CDC estimates that half of the approximately 20 million new STD infections each year occur in young people, ages 15-24. And, a significant number of these occur in people younger than 20. Another way of looking at this epidemic is to note that one in four teen girls is infected with one of the most common STDs. And, while the consequences of STDs may not be as obvious as the injuries caused by auto accidents, the physical and emotional effects can be more serious and long-lasting.

In this chapter, we will review the most common and serious STDs that affect teens and why it's so important that parents and teens are well-informed about them. Parents and teens frequently receive information about STDs from different sources, including their health care providers, sex-ed classes at school, and the Internet. Unfortunately, studies show that some of the information presented on the Web is inaccurate. For example, a recent survey of Internet sites found that 31% of sites included in the study incorrectly stated that herpes could not be transmitted by kissing an infected person. It can.

Becoming more knowledgeable about STDs is an important first step toward curbing an epidemic that is turning our teens' world upside down. To get started, let's take a short true/false quiz to help assess your knowledge about common STDs.

1. The most common bacterial STD among teens is gonorrhea. (true, false)

2. The most common viral STD among teens is herpes. (true, false)

3. Human papillomavirus (HPV) is more common in girls than boys. (true, false)

4. Most STDs in females cause obvious symptoms. (true, false)

5. Teens will be 100% protected against all STDs if condoms are used. (true, false)

6. The immature development of a teen's cervix places her at higher risk of being infected with chlamydia. (true, false)

7. AIDS (acquired immunodeficiency syndrome) cases, which are caused by HIV (human immunodeficiency virus), are becoming much less common in the teen population. (true, false)

8. Trichomoniasis is a very serious infection that has no cure. (true, false)

9. Hepatitis B is a viral infection of the liver which can be spread by sex. (true, false)

10. Chlamydia is the only STD that can be transmitted by oral sex. (true, false)

Answers

1. False. The most common bacterial infection among teens is chlamydia.

2. False. The most common viral infection among teens is HPV.

3. False. HPV is very common in both sexes. And, studies suggest that the HPV prevalence (number of people who have the infection at any given time) among males is at least as high as that among women.

4. False. Most STDs have no symptoms in females. For this reason, they often go undetected and untreated for a long time. When this happens, STDs are more likely to lead to serious complications.

5. False. Even in the best-case scenarios, condoms are not 100% effective in preventing STDs. Condoms can break, slip off, or be used incorrectly. And, with certain infections such as HPV or herpes, the presence of these viruses on the scrotum and base or lowest part of the penis, which are not covered by a condom, can lead to infection.

6. True. The teenage cervix is immature and has more mucus-producing tissue at its center. Having more exposed mucus-producing tissue increases the likelihood that a chlamydia infection will occur if the teen is exposed to the bacteria.

7. According to the Centers for Disease Control and Prevention (CDC), cases of AIDS among 13- to 19-year olds have risen significantly since 1985.

8. False. Trichomoniasis is caused by what is known as an intracellular parasite. It's neither a bacteria nor a virus. The parasite lives inside the lining of a teen girl's vagina or in the lining of the urethra (opening that drains

urine) in a teen girl or boy. It often causes a bothersome vaginal discharge and irritation. However, it does not cause serious illness and can be treated successfully with antibiotics.

9. True. Hepatitis B is a viral infection of the liver and is most commonly spread by sex in teens.

10. False. Many STDs have been shown to be transmitted by oral sex. These include chlamydia, gonorrhea, herpes, HIV, and HPV.

Teens are at very high risk for many STDs. They are also at increased risk for being infected soon after they begin having sex. Some of the reasons for this are:

- They are more likely to have unprotected sex (no condoms).

- They are more likely to have multiple partners over shorter periods of time.

- As mentioned in question 6, the teen cervix has more mucus-producing cells over a wider area as compared to older women. These mucus-producing cells make it easier for bacteria to attach to and cause an infection in the cervix. This is known to be a factor in the ease of transmission for chlamydia and gonorrhea infections.

- They have a more immature immune system, meaning their body is less able to fight infections.

- They are less likely to receive regular health care and receive prevention education.

In the next section, we'll discuss bacterial, viral, and other common STDs that teens are at risk for. In reviewing these STDs, it will be helpful to keep in mind that both bacterial and viral infections can be treated with medications. Bacterial infections can often be cured with medications. However, medications do not cure viral infections but serve to suppress the virus (keep it in check) or reduce its symptoms.

Bacterial STDs

1. Chlamydia

Chlamydia is the most common reportable bacterial STD in the country. Its rate of infection in teens is epidemic. Teenage girls, ages 15 to19, have very high rates of chlamydia.

Chlamydia can result in tremendous complications for teen girls and, to a lesser extent, for boys. It is spread through vaginal-penile, penile-anal, and oral sex. Chlamydia is often a *silent infection*. According to the CDC, three out of four females and one out of two males infected with chlamydia have absolutely no symptoms. Therefore, it infects the body and can do harm without its victim being aware.

Chlamydia infection symptoms include:

- An unusual vaginal or penile discharge

- Burning during urination (both sexes)

- Spotting blood in between periods or after sex

Chlamydia is easily diagnosed by collecting and testing secretions from a girl's cervix, vagina, or urethra, from the urethra of a boy's penis, or from a sample of urine.

The treatment for uncomplicated chlamydia is simple, and consists of a one-day or seven-day course of antibiotics. Because teens are at high risk for recurrence of this infection, repeat testing three months after the initial treatment is recommended.

Serious complications can result from chlamydia. Health professionals worry about this, and all parents and teens need to clearly understand the potential for these complications. They result primarily from **pelvic inflammatory disease (PID).** Pelvic inflammatory disease can occur when the chlamydia bacteria spreads from the cervix to the fallopian tubes and damages the lining of the fallopian tubes. This is the underlying reason for the most serious problems resulting from PID.

Complications of PID include:

- Tubal (ectopic) pregnancy

With an ectopic pregnancy, the embryo (very early pregnancy) starts to grow in the fallopian tube instead of the uterus. This can cause the fallopian tube to rupture and profuse bleeding may occur, even death. Rates of tubal pregnancy are reported to be *seven to 10 times higher* in teen girls/women who have had PID.

In the worst cases I have witnessed, teen girls were transported to the hospital by ambulance after passing out from blood loss after the fallopian tube ruptured. These girls not only required emergency surgery, but blood transfusions as well.

The shock of a teen girl's unintended pregnancy is greatly compounded by this life-threatening emergency.

- Abscess involving the ovary and fallopian tube

I clearly recall Vanida, a 16-year-old girl who was admitted to the hospital with severe abdominal pain. Vanida was ultimately diagnosed with an abscess of her fallopian tube. This means that her fallopian tube was enlarged and filled with pus. Even though Vanida's fallopian tube did not have to be removed, as is sometimes the case, it was clearly damaged and she would always be at high risk for the other complications of PID.

Her case was made more complex by the fact that she wouldn't admit to having had sex until several days after she was hospitalized. This made it more difficult for her health care staff to make a quick diagnosis and to provide the most optimal treatment. This case provides only one example of how a scared and perhaps conflicted teen can interfere with her health care.

- Infertility (inability to become pregnant)

Think for just a moment of the following scenario. A 15-year-old girl has unprotected sex and is infected with chlamydia. She initially has no symptoms and therefore doesn't seek early treatment. Later, she develops PID and her fallopian tubes are damaged. Fast forward 15 years when she and her husband try desperately to have a child but can't. They see a specialist who informs them that her damaged fallopian tubes are the problem. The only way they can have a child is to undergo extensive and very expensive surgical procedures. The couple is emotionally devastated, as they want a child more than anything and don't have the money to pay for expensive infertility treatments.

Unfortunately, this scenario is all too real. Studies show that women with a history of PID have a *10 times higher risk* of infertility.

• Chronic pelvic pain

This complication can be tremendously disabling. I have cared for several young women with severe and chronic pain, requiring large doses of pain medications and sometimes requiring surgery to remove their fallopian tubes, ovaries, and uterus. As many as *one in five* women with PID may ultimately experience chronic pelvic pain.

2. Gonorrhea

Gonorrhea is much less common than chlamydia. However, of those infected, teen girls ages 15 to 19 have the highest rates along with 20- to 24-year-old women.

Like chlamydia, gonorrhea can be spread by vaginal-penile, anal, and oral sex. And, it is diagnosed just like chlamydia. In the majority of cases, gonorrhea is also *silent*.

Gonorrhea symptoms include:

• Vaginal or penile discharge

• Vaginal bleeding between periods

• Pain with urination in teen girls and boys

- Itching, soreness, bleeding, and pain in the anal region (if anal sex occurs)

- Sore throat with discharge (if oral sex occurs)

Like chlamydia, gonorrhea can also cause PID and all the complications discussed above. Those infected with gonorrhea can experience spread of the bacteria through the bloodstream and develop unusual pains in the joints and a significant rash throughout their body.

Gonorrhea is treated with antibiotics. Health care providers frequently treat anyone infected with gonorrhea for chlamydia as well. This is because many teens infected with gonorrhea are often also infected with chlamydia.

3. Syphilis

Syphilis is one of the least common STDs in teens. However, if it does occur and goes untreated, its effects can be horrific.

Syphilis is caused by an unusual appearing bacteria which has a spiral shape. It can be spread through contact with infected body fluids or secretions from sores through vaginal, anal, or oral sex and during pregnancy. Syphilis is usually diagnosed through simple blood tests.

Syphilis infections are characterized by different stages which are:

- Primary syphilis

This stage is marked by an open sore, known as a chancre. This usually appears near where the infection was contracted. These sores can appear between 10–90 days after the person is exposed and usually heal on their own within three to six weeks. In addition, swollen lymph nodes are common.

- Secondary syphilis

This may appear about four to 10 weeks later if the primary syphilis is not treated. During this stage, an infected person often develops a severe rash, enlarged lymph nodes, fever, headache, and sore throat.

- Tertiary or late syphilis

This is very rare in the U.S., although when it does occur it is more likely in people infected with HIV. Late syphilis can infect any organ in the body and cause severe damage to the brain, heart, or other organs and can lead to death.

Fortunately, syphilis can be treated successfully with antibiotics and no significant harm need occur if it is detected and treated early.

Viral STDs

1. Human Papillomavirus (HPV)

HPV is the most common STD in the world, and it is especially prevalent in adolescents and young adults. Studies show that within three years after first having sex, 50% of young women who are tested will have positive results for HPV. Most people infected with HPV don't even know that they have it.

HPV is perhaps the most confusing, misunderstood, and anxiety-producing STD of our age. For one, the virus and the lesions it causes have been referred to by many different names. HPV has been called the genital wart virus, condyloma, and the virus that causes cervical cancer.

Second, HPV can trigger many different abnormalities in affected people. This is perhaps the most confusing aspect of the virus. Let's take a closer look at HPV.

The human papillomavirus is very small. It can infect the skin of the female's vulva (skin covering the external genital region), the lining of the vagina, and the cervix. In the male, it can infect the skin covering the penis and scrotum. In both females and males, HPV can infect the anus, the urethra (tube that carries urine from the bladder to the outside of the body) and, if oral sex occurs, the back of the throat (oropharynx). **HPV can be spread from one person to another by skin-to-skin contact.** This is an extremely important concept to understand. While HPV is transmitted by vaginal-penile sex, it can also be transmitted if a male's scrotum or penis are infected with the virus, and touch or rub against a female's vulva or outer genital area and vice versa.

I am frequently confronted with teen girls and adults as well, who are shocked to discover that they have HPV. They often report using condoms consistently and as instructed. In many situations, I have had to inform a very tearful teen that even though condoms were used when she had sex, they don't always prevent HPV. This is because condoms don't cover all areas which can be infected by HPV.

Consequences of HPV

- Genital warts

There are at least 40 different strains or types of HPV that can cause genital infections. HPV types 6 and 11 cause over 90% of genital warts. Approximately 1% of sexually active people have genital warts. Genital warts are very similar in appearance to the garden-variety warts that can appear on anyone's fingers or toes. The difference is that genital warts are confined to the genital regions listed at the beginning of this section on HPV.

One of the most striking incidences of HPV I ever encountered involved a case of genital warts in a patient, Amy, 18, a college freshman at a state university. I met Amy during my early days in practice. She came to my office with her mom because she had developed large growths in her genital area. She looked embarrassed and scared. During her exam, I found that most of Amy's genital area was covered with cauliflower-sized warts. She could barely sit down.

Treating Amy's warts required rather extensive laser surgery. However, repairing her self-esteem and easing her fears about carrying the HPV diagnosis wasn't that easy. Amy was infected by the first boy she had ever had sex with. At least with Amy, it was clear who gave her

HPV. With many girls, figuring out the transmission (who gave this to me?) is impossible, as we'll review at the end of this section.

Unlike Amy, most girls who develop the classic warts have smaller lesions on the vulva which can be easily treated with medications or minor procedures done in a health care provider's office.

- Abnormal changes in cells (dysplasia or intra-epithelial neoplasia)

In addition to causing obvious warts, HPV can stimulate the cells in the skin of the external genital region, the lining of the vagina, and cervix of females to appear abnormal when inspected with the aid of a magnifying instrument called a colposcope. These changes would be suspected if a female had an abnormal Pap or HPV test. New testing guidelines recommend delaying Pap and HPV testing until a girl reaches age 21. More information will be presented about these new guidelines in Chapter 8.

- Cervical cancer

HPV is often termed "the virus that causes cervical cancer." In all, approximately 70% of cervical cancers are thought to be caused by HPV types 16 and 18. Because a girl/woman would need to have abnormal changes in her cervical cells for several years before she would develop cervical cancer, this disease is extremely rare in teens.

- Other cancers

Cervical cancer is the most common cancer triggered by infection with HPV. However, HPV is also considered a risk factor for the development of certain vulvar and vaginal cancers in females, anal and throat cancers in females and males, and penile cancers in males.

3 Most Commonly Asked Questions About HPV

How Did I Get It?

The simplest answer is that it was contracted by having sex with someone else who has HPV. The truth of the matter is that HPV is exceedingly common and avoiding it is very difficult. As a matter of fact, most sexually active people will be infected with HPV over the course of their lifetime.

There are three basic ways to become infected with HPV:

1. Penile-vaginal or penile-anal sex.

2. Any activity in which the male genitals (penis/scrotum) come into contact with the female's external genital area. This is sometimes referred to as "outercourse," although teens don't generally use that term. And, if a girl has HPV on her vulva, finger touching of this area can spread the HPV to her vagina, anus, or cervix.

3. Oral sex. HPV can lead to infection at the back of the throat (oropharynx). However, this type of spread seems to be rare.

Is My Partner Cheating on Me?

My patients who have been diagnosed with HPV regularly ask this question. The only way cheating could be determined to be the likely cause of infection is if both partners were virgins when the sexual relationship began and then later, one partner (almost always the girl), was diagnosed with HPV.

Otherwise, there is no way to tell if your current partner has been unfaithful. This is because most HPV infections are silent. Therefore, the majority of people who have HPV don't even know it and they can infect other people without having a clue. And, HPV is very highly infectious—exposure to the virus means a high chance of developing an infection with the virus. In fact, the odds of contracting HPV after sex with an infected person are 40%. Think of its behavior as akin to the common cold virus—if you come into contact with someone who's sick, you're very likely to get sick as well.

The bottom line is that if a person has had sex with more than one person, it's impossible to be 100% sure where the infection came from.

Is There a Cure for HPV?

No, there is not a cure, but the good news is that the vast majority of new HPV infections will resolve spontaneously. However, remember that there are many types of HPV, and reinfection with another HPV type is still possible. You'll learn more about prevention of HPV, including the HPV vaccine, in Chapter 8.

2. Genital Herpes Simplex Virus (HSV)

There was a time when infection with the herpes virus was considered a horrible and dreaded consequence of sex. Back then, human papillomavirus (HPV) and human immunodeficiency virus (HIV) were barely detectable on the radar screen as important viral diseases. Now, despite the stigma and physical symptoms that can result from a herpes infection, the fact that it is rarely associated with life-threatening illness makes it much less frightening.

Like HPV, most people who have the herpes virus (HSV) don't know it because they lack symptoms.

Findings of HSV include:

- Painful blisters on the vulva or anal skin (teen girls) and on the penis, scrotum, or anal skin (teen boys)

- Open sores caused when the blisters pop (which usually resolve in two to four weeks)

- Fevers, chills, and other flu-like symptoms (usually with the first outbreak)

- Recurrent episodes of the blisters and open sores

To confirm the diagnosis of a genital herpes infection, the health care provider takes a swab from the sore and cultures it. Blood testing may be recommended in some situations.

One of the complications that can result from a severe herpes outbreak is scarring. I recall the case of Jackie, a 16-year-old girl who came to my office complaining of discomfort in her vulvar area. She had been diagnosed with a severe herpes infection a few weeks earlier. When I examined Jackie, it was obvious that she had developed significant scarring because of her infection. The labia (often called "the lips") of the vulva which are supposed to be open and free on both sides were sealed together in Jackie. This occurs when open herpes lesions cause oozing and, in some patients, the continued oozing causes the skin on both sides of the vulva to stick together. In Jackie's case, medication was used to try and separate the skin. However, this proved unsuccessful and Jackie required surgery.

I want to make a point here, parents. Teens need to understand that catching an STD can be pretty awful, but they might be one of those unlucky enough to require hospital care and surgery. Intimate relationships can have significant consequences.

Then, there are the emotional aspects. Practically without exception, every teen or young woman that I've had to break the news to about a herpes infection has been emotionally devastated. This is consistent with studies that show psychological distress is often associated with a new diagnosis of herpes.

After a diagnosis like this, teens have a wake-up call that they now have something that will be with them for life. They'll need to tell any future partners about this and warn them that they could be at risk for a herpes infection. The painful nature of this disease also seems to contribute to the heavy psychological burden. The good news here is that as time goes on, infections tend to be less and less painful.

Here are some other important facts about genital herpes infections:

- HSV infections have been diagnosed in one out of five adolescents and adults.

- There are two types of herpes viruses, HSV-1 and HSV-2. Genital herpes has usually been associated with type 2. Type 1 herpes, the common cause of cold sores, or blisters on the lips or in the mouth, is being detected more frequently in genital herpes outbreaks. This is most likely the result of oral sex. It's important to remember that herpes infections, both HSV-1 and HSV-2, can be transmitted through oral sex.

- Herpes infections can be deadly in babies who are infected during birth. This is why mothers with known herpes sores at the time of labor undergo cesarean section.

- Teen girls who have genital herpes (HSV-2) are at higher risk of being infected with HIV if they are exposed.

Teens diagnosed with herpes can be treated with antiviral medications. But remember, medication does not cure herpes; it only helps to decrease the severity and length of symptoms.

3. Human Immunodeficiency Virus (HIV)

HIV, the virus that causes AIDS (acquired immunodeficiency syndrome), remains the most feared of all.

A person can live with HIV for many years before symptoms develop. A person infected with HIV develops AIDS when he or she comes down with one of the serious infections or illnesses associated with HIV. This incubation period for AIDS—the time it takes for a person infected with HIV to develop AIDS—is about 10 to 12 years. It is estimated that a large portion of adults who have AIDS were infected with HIV when they were teenagers.

Without exception, people diagnosed with HIV react with a deep sense of pain, dread, and sadness. This is still true, even though HIV/AIDS does not equal almost certain death, as was often the case before the development of effective drugs to halt its progress. Consider the following comments from teenagers who learned that they were infected with HIV:

"I was devastated, thought I was going to kill myself. Sometimes I just feel like giving up."

—Audrey, age 17

"I'm young and don't know of anybody living with the disease. Hardly even the one who gave it to me. He was 21 and took advantage. I have a young heart, but an old soul."

—15-year-old from Hawaii

"I felt crushed, like my life was over … like I was nobody. I thought I was going to die real soon. Every day, I ask myself, 'Why me?'"

—H., age 17

Fortunately, most teens learn how to live with HIV and lead productive lives as long as they receive good medical care and continue to take their medications as prescribed. As far as the emotional consequences, most teens also learn how to cope with fear, anxiety, and dread. They share their stories in the hope that other teens will become more knowledgeable about HIV/AIDS and avoid the risks.

What does every teen need to know about HIV/AIDS?

- HIV is most commonly diagnosed by blood testing; however, it can also be diagnosed on fluid obtained from the mouth or urine. Antiviral medications can help people infected with HIV live longer and healthier lives, but there is no cure for HIV.

- Most people with HIV infection don't know that they have it. It is estimated that over 50% of HIV-infected teens do not know they are infected. There are no clues from looking at a person that she/he has HIV.

Considering this estimate, it's no wonder that teens are among the fastest-growing groups with HIV infection. This is an extremely important fact to get across to teens.

And, even if teens know they are infected with HIV, there's no guarantee that a young person will share this information with his or her sex partner. Teens may be too scared or embarrassed—no matter how selfish this may seem.

- You don't get HIV by hugging or shaking hands with someone who is infected.

And, it isn't caught by coming into contact with toilet seats or doorknobs. HIV is spread by sexual fluids or blood. Therefore, if you have sex with an infected person without the protection of a condom, or share needles used by an infected person, you can get HIV.

- Oral sex is not safe sex.

As we learned in Chapter 2, many teens participate in oral sex so this fact causes particular concern. While it's true that teens' risk of contracting HIV is higher when they have vaginal or anal sex with an infected person, numerous studies have shown that HIV can be transmitted through oral sex. Not having sex is the only way for a person to completely guarantee that he or she won't get HIV. The next best way to prevent HIV is not to have sex with anyone unless he or she has tested negative for HIV, to use condoms, and for both partners not to have sex with anyone else.

- HIV/AIDS is not a gay person's disease.

HIV can infect anyone who comes into intimate contact with this virus. It does not discriminate among sex, race, class, country of origin, age, or any other dividing line. It is true that men who have sex with men, intravenous drug users, African-Americans, and Hispanics are disproportionately affected by HIV/AIDS. The majority of new HIV infections in young people occur among gay and bisexual African-American males, followed by gay and bisexual Hispanic and non-Hispanic white males.

4. Hepatitis B

Hepatitis B is a disease of the liver caused by the hepatitis B virus (HBV). Of all the different types of hepatitis, hepatitis B is the one usually transmitted by sex. It can also be spread in other ways, including drug use that involves sharing needles, during pregnancy and delivery, or by sharing items like toothbrushes with an infected person. The virus can live outside of the body for days and still cause someone to be infected. In this way, hepatitis is very different from the other viruses we've discussed.

Hepatitis B is diagnosed by blood testing. Many HBV infections are silent.

Hepatitis B infection symptoms include:

- Jaundice (a yellow coloring of the skin)

- A light color to the stool

- Fever, nausea and vomiting

- Fatigue, poor appetite

Most people will clear the hepatitis virus and experience no serious problems. Some people will continue to carry the virus in the blood, but won't show any obvious signs of the infection. These people are called "carriers" of the virus. They can infect other people. A smaller percentage of people will develop cirrhosis (damage to the liver), liver cancer, and possibly death.

How does hepatitis B affect teens?

- Most teens who are infected with the hepatitis B virus get it through sex with a partner of the opposite sex.

- Risk factors include more than one sex partner in the previous six months and/or a history of having other STDs.

- Asian and Pacific Islander teens are at highest risk.

The good news is that hepatitis B infections are decreasing in the U.S. Most of this decrease is due to the administration of the hepatitis B vaccine to young people. More information about preventing hepatitis B will be presented in Chapter 8.

5. Trichomoniasis

Lastly, I'll review a common, but much less serious, infection, trichomoniasis. This is pronounced "trick oh mo NYE a sis," which is sometimes shortened to just "trich."

Trichomoniasis infection symptoms include:

- A foul-smelling vaginal discharge

- Vaginal itching and burning

- Burning with urination

- Teen boys often have no symptoms

A trichomoniasis infection is usually diagnosed by inspection of a swab of the teen girl's vaginal discharge or a teen male's urethral discharge under a microscope. The treatment is simple, consisting of antibiotics which may be taken by mouth or a cream or gel inserted into the vagina.

One important note about trichomoniasis is that it can increase the risk of premature labor in a pregnant teen or woman. Therefore, its diagnosis and treatment are very important in anyone who is pregnant.

STDs and Race

Minority teens face higher risks for most of the STDs we have discussed. African-Americans, and to a lesser extent Hispanics, are disproportionately affected by these infections. HPV seems less associated with race than the other STDs, though this is an area that has not been studied extensively.

The epidemic of HIV in minority populations is especially disturbing. In its efforts to reduce the incidence of HIV, particularly in communities at highest risk, the CDC promotes initiatives such as the Minority AIDS Initiative (http:minorityhealth.hhs.gov/templates/browse.aspx?lvl=2&lvlID=36).

I urge parents, educators, health care workers, and all concerned about teen sexual health to maintain a heightened sense of urgency about the challenges affecting communities disproportionately impacted by HIV and other STDs.

Chapter 5

Talking with and Guiding Your Teen About Sex: What Parents Really Need to Know

It takes a village to raise a child.

—ancient African proverb

This is what I know for sure about talking with and guiding teens about sex—with the right information and support, you can help your teen make respectful, responsible and healthy decisions. As discussed in Chapter 1, so many parents feel uneasy about this task. According to the National Campaign to Prevent Teen and Unplanned Pregnancy, nine out of ten parents believe they should talk to their kids about sex, but don't know what to say, how to say it, or when to start.

We don't receive formal training on how to talk with and educate our kids about sex. Parenting expert Dr. Michael Popkin comments, "For every other job in our society that is difficult and important, you get some kind of training." That's what you'll accomplish in reading this chapter: your personal training program on clarifying your values, making them clear to your teen, and laying the foundation for an ongoing dialogue.

Even if you feel uncertain about your ability to talk to and guide your child through the transitional teen years, **you can do it!** As noted in Chapter 1, you have already mastered many parenting skills, and you can refine and build on those skills to talk with your teen about sex. ***Never forget that parents are the primary sex educators of their children.*** Parents make a tremendous difference in the choices their teens make and play a pivotal role in helping them avoid teen pregnancy and STDs. The key lies in developing a level of comfort in communicating your beliefs and values about sexuality and sexual behavior to your teen, accurately and naturally.

You are perfectly capable of doing this and, if you are already talking with your teen about sex, you can practice and improve your skill much like a professional athlete who continually strives to do better. Remember that there are plenty of resources available to assist you—you don't have to go it alone. Seek support from health care professionals, teachers, family, and friends. It really does take a village to raise a child.

Values Clarification

To guide your teen effectively, it's important to do two things initially. First, becoming a well-informed parent is critical, and much of this book is dedicated to guaranteeing that you have all the important information you need. Second, clarifying and understanding your beliefs and values about teen sexuality and behavior is also essential. Sexuality plays an important role in our lives and should be embraced positively. Your belief about when it becomes appropriate or acceptable to engage in sexual displays of affection is very personal, as is how you guide your teen. The advice I offer is meant to help you think this through and articulate what you mean.

What do you *really* think about teens and sex? The following short quiz will help you clarify your beliefs and values, which is very important in communicating your expectations to your teen. There are no right or wrong answers. What's important is that you spend some time thinking about these issues to gain insight into your own views.

1. Which of the following statements **most closely** reflects your beliefs?

    a. Teens should wait until they are adults and married to have sex.

    b. Teens should wait until they are adults and married to have sex, but I don't think this is realistic.

c. Teens should wait until they are at least 18 to have sex.

d. It is OK for teens at least 16 years old to have sex, as long as they are in a committed/monogamous relationship and responsible enough to protect themselves against pregnancy and STDs.

2. Which of the following factors is **most important** in determining your values with respect to teens and sexual behavior?

a. The values you were raised with

b. The information you obtain from newspapers, magazines, books, TV, the Internet, and other media

c. The teachings of your religious faith

d. The values of your spouse, close friends, and family members

e. None of the above

3. The **most important** thing parents can do to help teens delay sexual activity is:

a. Warn them about the risks of becoming pregnant and of the hardships that teen parents often face

b. Warn them about the risks of contracting an STD and the dangers of STDs

c. Consistently demonstrate love and support and create an environment where their child feels comfortable asking them about sex

d. Support comprehensive sex education in the school system

4. Which statement **most closely reflects** how you feel about your own sexual behavior when you were a teen?

   a. I feel that I was way too young when I started having sex and later regretted it.

   b. I waited until I was 18 or older to have sex and don't regret it.

   c. I did not have a boyfriend/girlfriend when I was a teen, did not have sex, and feel comfortable with this.

   d. I had a steady boyfriend/girlfriend during my teen years, but did not have sex because I did not believe in sex before marriage.

5. Which of the following displays of affection do you think is OK for unmarried teens?

   a. Hugging, kissing on the lips

   b. Oral sex

   c. Mutual masturbation—fondling of breasts, touching of penis and vaginal area

   d. French kissing

   e. Anal sex

   f. Penile-vaginal sex (standard definition of sex)

   g. None of the above

   h. All of the above

6. Which of the following statements do you agree with **most strongly**?

   a. Teen sex should always be strongly discouraged.

   b. Teen sex should be discouraged for those under 18 only.

    c. Teens who are having sex should be told that what they are doing is risky and can lead to pregnancy and STDs.

    d. Teens who are having sex should be taken to a health care provider for birth control and STD testing.

Giving thoughtful consideration to these questions will help you to develop a better understanding of what you really feel is appropriate dating/sexual behavior for teens. You will have opened the door to creating a more open, honest, and direct approach to talking with and guiding your child. Next, I'll share the observations from my clinical and seminar experiences, and identify helpful parenting tools on talking with your teen. You might find that as you prepare to talk with your teen, some of your beliefs and values may change, and that's OK, too.

Observations and Comments

The standard advice on talking with your kids about sex emphasizes the importance of starting the conversation early. Your preschooler may have asked, "Where do babies come from?" giving you the opportunity to demonstrate an open, easygoing, and comfortable approach to talking about the basics of sex. The questions usually become more complex as the child grows: "What is a penis?" "What does oral sex mean?" "How do people get AIDS? Can I get it?"

While conversations with your children about sex should begin when your child is very young, don't worry if you haven't done that. It's not too late! You can start now and continue this conversation until your child is an adult.

In my ob/gyn practice and during my many years supervising a Teen Pregnancy and STD Prevention Program, I have had many opportunities to learn, gain insight, and form opinions about the most helpful information for parents seeking to better guide their teens toward healthy choices about sex.

The Top 3 Parent Concerns About Teen Sex

While no two parents are exactly alike in philosophy or outlook, in my experience most parents share common concerns about teens and sex. These are the three most common I have heard from parents, and my recommendations on how best to address them.

1. How Do I Communicate More Effectively with My Teen About Sex?

Parents want their teens to feel comfortable talking to them about sex. According to a survey by the National Campaign to Prevent Teen Pregnancy titled "With One Voice," 91% of adults said it would be easier for teens to postpone sexual activity and prevent teen pregnancy if they were able to discuss this topic with their parents. In order for teens to feel comfortable talking with their parents about sex and asking them for advice, the parent must have communication skills that promote understanding.

Think back on your own teen years. Were you less likely to share sensitive concerns with your parents than when you were a young child? Let's face it, teens tend to spend more time interacting with and conversing with their peers than with their parents. And, sometimes parent-teen communication can seem downright impossible. Do you recognize any of the following scenarios?

- Your teen talks incessantly on the phone with her girlfriends but can barely muster one-syllable responses to any of your questions.

- When you question your teen about the date she went on last night her response is, "You're always trying to get into my business!"

- Your teen is fond of saying, "You just don't understand!"

If so, you might be thinking, "What's a parent supposed to do?" The truth is that the fundamentals of communicating with your teen about sex are no different from the sound principles you use to communicate effectively with anyone.

First of all, as discussed in Chapter 1, parents can focus on the positive when talking with their teen. Think about it. Are you motivated to communicate with someone who frequently criticizes or nags you? And, it's important to focus on the **issue** and not the **individual** when dealing with difficult subjects.

Parents are human and sometimes make comments that do little to build good communication with their teens. One parent I encountered used this admonition to tell her teen son to delay sex: "Don't put that thing (penis) anywhere it doesn't belong!" Although I'm sure that this parent meant well, this type of language does little to create the type of environment in which your teen will listen to your message or want to come to you with questions and for advice.

Let's take a look at how this comment could have been worded differently: "Son, I'm so proud of how well you're doing in school and the way you help me with your younger brother. You do so many things well. But I have some concerns about how things are going with you and your girlfriend. I've been reading about the numbers of teens who are having sex. You know that as your mother I'm always concerned about you, and I really want to stress the importance of your waiting to have sex."

While this is only one of hundreds of scripts she could have chosen, this opening demonstrates some of the key ingredients for establishing effective communication with your teen:

- Focuses on the positive and compliments her son before mentioning what is troubling her

- Uses the word "I," instead of "you" to relay that she's speaking from her point of view and not trying to speak for her son

- Expresses her concern about the problem of teen sex in a general way as opposed to criticizing on her son individually; she challenges the behavior, not the person

- Couches what she really wants him to hear, (i.e., waiting to have sex), in a layer of concern

I want to stress this last point. **Always seek to communicate love and caring in your conversations with your teen**. Teens who feel confident to the core that their parent deeply loves them will know that the message you are delivering is ultimately in their best interest. This doesn't mean that you won't get an exasperated "Oh, Mom" or hear "I don't need to be told…." The key is that your message will have been heard, and your teen will be much more likely to think about and strongly consider what you have said.

2. How Can I Get My Teen to Come to Me with Questions/Concerns About Sex?

Chances are your teen has no trouble coming to you for money. If only your daughter or son could come to you as readily with concerns, questions, or even fears about sex, or for your take on how to handle any issues about dating or relationships. While some parents and teens may have that near-perfect, open relationship that allows them to discuss sensitive issues like sex easily, my experience has been that most don't. This is one of the most common sentiments I hear from parents. What can parents do to make their teens feel comfortable about **approaching** them with dating- or sex-related issues?

There are many key tools or traits that will make you an **Approachable Parent** who lets your teen feel safe and comfortable in bringing concerns to you. The top seven traits listed below are primarily based on my direct work with teens and their parents.

1. A Listening Ear

What are some characteristics of good listeners?

- They let the other person do the talking. We all know what it's like to try to have a conversation with someone when it's hard to get a word in edgewise.

- They are attentive and listen actively. They nod their head or say "yes" or "um hm" to show that they are very involved in what you are saying.

- They use eye contact and look at the person who's talking, as opposed to the TV, a Blackberry or cell phone, or the magazine they were reading.

- They don't interrupt, but respond when the other person is finished talking.

- Remember that when you are having a conversation with your teen, do as much, if not more, listening as talking. Remember to ask your teen, "What do you think about that? or "How do you see this?" Even if your teen responds with an opinion that disturbs you— "oral sex is no big deal"—be careful not to dismiss what your teen has said. You can simply say, "I don't see it that way," or "I disagree." And then tell your teen why you feel the way you do.

2. A Nonjudgmental Outlook

This might be a bit difficult for many parents to swallow. After all, you are the parent so don't you get to judge? If you find out your 14-year-old teen has been having sex, how are you supposed to react? How parents react internally to a discovery like this will vary. Being nonjudgmental doesn't mean that you don't get to have an opinion or to be upset. What it means is that you don't react externally by condemning or berating your teen. In this instance, you might choose to say something like "I'm not very happy about this. I think it's time we sit down and talk about this issue." A judgmental response might go something like, "How could you do this? That's really stupid on your part!"

The underlying feelings may be identical, whether the response is judgmental or nonjudgmental. The difference is that a judgmental response is more likely to leave your teen feeling ashamed and abandoned. A nonjudgmental response is more likely to leave your teen feeling that she or he can really talk to you and that even if you're unhappy, you're going to help in dealing with the situation.

3. Flexibility

The elements of trust and confidentiality are very important traits of an approachable parent. Sometimes this requires flexibility and the willingness to consider several options. I've encountered situations where a teen girl shares information about dating and sex with her mother, but doesn't want her father to know. This is a very sensitive topic and there are different ways to approach it. One suggestion for a parent's response is, "I'd love to be able to promise you that I won't discuss whatever you have to say with your dad, but there are some things I wouldn't want to hide from him. Instead, why don't we talk about what the issue is and then decide how we can best deal with it?" Perhaps the teen has something personal to confide like, "I just started my period for the first time." A mother could probably agree to keep this to herself until her daughter felt comfortable letting her dad know. On the other hand, if a teen says she let a friend take nude photos of her and they've been posted on a website, her mother might determine that her husband needs to be informed.

I've also encountered teens who are comfortable talking about sex-related topics with a favorite aunt, but not with their parents. How parents and relatives handle this differs. What matters most is for teens to have absolute trust in their parent or other responsible adult when they choose to share personal information.

I strongly urge parents to be open to their teens talking to another close relative or a responsible adult about sex-related questions. I've seen parents react with hurt or anger at the thought of their teen turning to someone else. I completely understand the feeling—we'd all like to think our children would come to us first. But the primary concern is that your teen is able to talk to a responsible adult who can give accurate information. Never lose sight of this!

4. Warmth

> *No man can be a good teacher unless he has feelings of **warm** affections toward his pupils and a genuine desire to impart to them what he believes to be of value.*

> —Bertrand Russell, English logician and philosopher, 1872-1970

This quote holds true for parents and their children, too. A warm and loving attitude is a welcoming one. However, in our busy and stressful lives, it's easy to lose sight of this very simple concept. Creating a warm atmosphere will help you to be an approachable parent for your teen. Doing this can be as simple as giving your teen a hug when he comes home tired after a long day at school.

5. A Calm Demeanor

When there's a storm brewing, a major catastrophe, or any kind of emergency, what do we crave from those in authority? Calm reactions.

It's always more helpful to be calm in the midst of a storm or a crisis, rather than to react with anger, frenzy, or hysterics. How would you respond if your 16-year-old daughter told you she was pregnant? Remember, I'm asking you how you would respond, which is not the same as asking how you would feel. Remaining calm in this situation is not the same as burying your feelings and not showing disappointment. A calm demeanor will help you and your teen to deal with what's really important and to take more logical and meaningful steps in handling the situation.

For instance, if your 16-year-old-daughter told you she was pregnant, a calm response might sound like this: "This is very difficult news for me to hear. I'm going to need a few moments to gather my thoughts together before we talk."

6. Lightheartedness

As they say, "Laughter is the best medicine." Maintaining a sense of humor, especially during the teen years, can be difficult. But a sense of humor will make it much more likely that your teen will come to you when he or she needs help or advice. The truth is that while early teen sex, teen pregnancy, and STDs are serious issues, teen dating and relationships give us plenty to joke about. During the Teen Pregnancy Prevention Seminars that I organized, many humorous moments occurred during role-playing between parents and unrelated teens. Having a good sense of humor in general makes it easier to deal with any sensitive issue, not just sex.

7. Open-Mindedness

A teen who already knows what your response is going to be might have a "why bother?" attitude about going to you in the first place. Having a rigid or inflexible mentality will interfere with your desire to be an approachable parent. We all have examples in our own lives of rigid people who were very difficult to deal with. Think of the boss who won't consider a flexible schedule for an employee who's been working for the company for 10 years and has a unique need, or the coach who was so rigid that he wouldn't allow his players to have water even when the temperature outside reached 105.

By communicating an open mind, you give your teen the comfort of knowing that whatever the issue, you will hear it and a discussion will take place before a decision is made. Isn't this what we all want from those in authority?

To be approachable, be the type of parent that you'd like to have. It's really that simple.

3. How Can I Prevent My Teen from Having Sex?

You probably already know the answer to this question: **You can't**. That's right, there's absolutely nothing that you can do to prevent your teen from having sex. What you can do is to take steps to decrease the likelihood that your teen will have sex or increase the chances that he or she will delay having sex. You can't be with your teen 24/7. At some point, parents have to trust their teen and know they have done everything in their power to educate him/her and to instill the values and beliefs that they hold dear.

This issue is one that I have come across several times. When parents ask me directly, "What can I do to prevent or make sure my child doesn't have sex?" I believe that they're signaling something that is difficult for many parents to accept. ***Parents do not have 100% control over their children or over any outcomes for the children.*** Even parents who have great relationships with their teens sometimes have a teen who has early sex, becomes pregnant, or contracts an STD. As with everything in life, there are no guarantees.

I've had parents ask me if there was some way I could secretly place their child on birth control and other parents joke about needing a chastity belt for their teen daughters. This is not the answer. I encourage you to keep in mind that your goal should be to do everything that you can to ***decrease the risk*** that your teen will make poor choices about sex. If you have a strong, open relationship with your teen, make certain your teen receives accurate sex education, and communicate your values clearly and consistently, then your teen is much less likely to succumb to risky sexual behavior.

Do Your Homework

When talking with your teen about dating, relationships, and your values about sex, it will be helpful to have considered what you really want to get across and how best to do this. The next **three sections** provide hints that will help you prepare for those meaningful conversations.

8 Things to Tell Yourself

1. I don't have to be perfect.

I believe that fear about "getting it wrong" is one of the biggest obstacles for parents in talking to their kids about sex. You don't have to be an expert to communicate effectively with your teen. And you're probably a lot more skilled than you think. My philosophy is that if you demonstrate a caring attitude, you're more than halfway there. And if you say something that you later regret, such as "You'll never amount to anything if you start having sex at your age," you can always approach your teen later with a more positive statement. You might say, "I really didn't mean what I said. It's just that I'm worried about you having sex, possibly getting pregnant, and not being able to accomplish your goal of going to college."

2. I have multiple opportunities to get my points across to my teen.

It's important to avoid trying to say everything you want to get across in one session or **"The Talk."** Teens consistently express that they cringe at the thought of "The Talk." Your goal should be to have many conversations about this issue, some planned, but many impromptu. Many teachable moments will arise both before and during the teen years. Be alert for them, and take advantage of as many as you can. For example, some notable celebrity teens have recently become teen parents. You can use these examples as ice breakers to discuss how you feel about teens having sex. This could then lead to a discussion about teen pregnancy and many of the hardships that teen parents face.

3. I am approachable.

Remember the 7 Traits of Approachable Parents: A listening ear, nonjudgmental outlook, flexibility, warmth, a calm demeanor, lightheartedness, and open-mindedness.

4. I know what I want to say first.

Practice makes perfect. It's absolutely fine to formulate your ideas first before approaching your child. You might even want to practice by saying things out loud to your imaginary child first. Even if a teachable moment arises suddenly, you can still take a few seconds to think about what you want to say before responding.

5. I remember my teen years.

Even under the best circumstances, talking with your teen about relationships, dating, or sex, can be a little awkward. If your teen seems uncomfortable, don't be surprised. Think back to your teen years. Did you have any talks with your parents about dating, relationships, and sex? If so, try to recall how you felt. If you didn't, just imagine how you would have felt.

6. Shorter can be better.

Your conversations don't have to be formal or lengthy to be helpful. For example, if you're watching TV with your teen, there might be a scenario involving a romantic teen relationship. This can present an opportunity to make a very simple comment like, "I like the fact that she makes time for having fun with her girlfriends and doesn't spend all her time with her boyfriend." By doing so, you make a point about balance in romantic relationships. Remember, it's about developing an ongoing dialogue, not about trying to cram everything you want to get across into one or two conversations.

7. Don't assume anything.

I've heard some parents make comments like, "Oh no, my daughter's not having sex—she doesn't even have a boyfriend." What that parent may not realize is that her daughter may have participated in oral group sex at a party last weekend or may feel pressured to have sex because she thinks "everyone is doing it."

Don't be afraid to ask your child, "Are you having sex? I mean any type of sex: oral, anal or vaginal?" or "I keep reading stats about the numbers of teens who are having sex. Have you felt pressure to have sex or even had sex?"

8. I communicate love and concern.

Your teen is very special to you, and you want the very best for him or her. If that weren't true, you wouldn't be reading this book. Your teen needs to feel this and to hear this as often as possible. How you express this may be even more important than what you express. Remember that a large part of communication is nonverbal. Your teen receives information from you through your gestures, facial expressions, and tone of voice just as much from the actual words that you speak. Be aware of your *nonverbal communication* and always seek to express love and concern to your teen.

8 Things to Say to Your Teen

This list will give you ideas about what you may wish to say to your teen. It is meant to serve as a guide only and is far from being exhaustive. The key here is to think about what you most want to get across to your teen about relationships, dating, and sex.

1. Respect yourself.

We teach our children to show respect to others. But how often do we tell our children to respect themselves? The importance of this message has been commented on by many parents and teens I have encountered. The message can be clear and simple, as one parent commented: "You have to respect yourself in order to be respected by others." A teen who has a high level of respect for herself/himself is much less likely to be swayed by peer pressure and much more likely to avoid risky behaviors, including alcohol or drug use and/or early sex.

A simple sentence is often cited to help teens demonstrate self-respect and deal better with peer pressure. If a teen boy says to a teen girl, "If you loved me you'd have sex with me," the teen girl responds, "If you loved me you wouldn't pressure me to have sex." This is the type of response that a girl with a strong sense of self-respect would likely choose to make.

2. Be responsible.

While teens are not adults, they should be encouraged to take responsibility for their actions. For instance, if you've allowed your teen to date at 16, she needs to be responsible enough to be home by her curfew time. If your teen has the privilege of driving your car, he should follow the rules of the road.

A responsible teen may not always follow your advice. However, responsible teens who have been adequately educated will make sure they are protected against pregnancy and STDs if they do have sex.

3. This is what I believe about teens and sex.

As noted earlier in this chapter, it's important to clarify your values about teen dating, relationships, and sex before you can impart those values to your child. If you absolutely believe that any sex outside of marriage is wrong, tell your teen this. It would also be helpful to explain why you feel this way, and what displays of affection you feel are appropriate for her/his age.

If you feel that sex should take place only within a committed relationship between adults 18 and older, tell your teen this. Most teens and adults support the view that sex within a committed relationship is most appropriate, according to surveys from the National Campaign to Prevent Teen Pregnancy.

Perhaps you have mixed feelings. You may prefer that your 17-year-old teen, who has been going steady with the same partner for a year, refrain from sex. However, you're concerned that she is at risk and you're even more concerned about your teen being protected against pregnancy and STDs. You may choose to express to your teen that while you do want her to refrain from sex, her safety is your primary concern. If she were to have sex it's very important that she also use birth control and condoms.

4. Make your own, independent decisions.

The most recent information from the National Youth Risk Behavior Surveillance Survey indicates that approximately six in 10 high school students have had sex by the time they graduated.

You can use this data to help your teen confront peer pressure to have sex. When I was growing up, the admonition was "Don't follow your friends, they may lead you off a cliff." Also, let your teen know that sometimes kids may talk to impress their friends, but may not be as sexually experienced as they portray themselves to be.

5. Don't rely on friends for advice about sex.

Friends are good for many things, but accurate information about sex is not one of them. I've had many teens in my office comment or ask questions about the information they got from their friends. Examples include, "I've heard that the birth control pill is really bad for your body and causes cancer," or "I was told that you really can't get pregnant if you're only 14." Chapter 7 describes several birth control myths that teens are susceptible to.

Every teen needs to receive accurate sexual health information from a reliable adult. While comprehensive sex education at school may be available for some, parents can and should be a key source for accurate information.

6. What you see on TV and in movies seldom reflects real life.

Teens need to be told that what they're seeing on TV and at the movies is often a far cry from what happens in real life. They probably don't see couples talking about birth control and they definitely don't see them using it before a sex scene on TV or in a movie. In real life, this behavior could lead to an unintended pregnancy and/or an STD.

7. Being a teen parent is really hard.

> *The pressures of being a parent are equal to any pressure on earth. To be a conscious parent, and really look to that little being's mental and physical health, is a responsibility which most of us, including me, avoid most of the time because it's too hard.*

—John Lennon, musician, 1940-1980

None of us really understands the monumental task of parenting until we become parents ourselves. Becoming a teen parent has all the additional hardships covered in Chapter 3. Tell your teen that it takes a tremendous amount of time and energy to successfully raise a child, not to mention money. Stress that it's important not to risk becoming a teen parent. Practically every teen parent I have interacted with has commented on the loss of freedom after having a child, the inability to hang out with their friends, and the difficulties involved in being a teen parent.

8. There's a difference between infatuation, love, and sex.

The distinctions between these words may seem very obvious to you as a parent, but to teens the differences may not be so apparent. Romantic relationships usually begin with infatuation—romantic feelings most often referred to as a "crush." Teens may mistake this infatuation for "true love" and think that what they are feeling will last forever. An infatuated teen may think that sex is OK since she/he is "in love." Unfortunately, once the infatuation ends, the teen may regret having acted based on just "feeling in love."

Definitions of romantic love are very individual and personal. Parents are in a unique position to help their children to learn what love is and what love isn't.

Parents can help their teen to understand that there are many ways to express love and caring in a romantic relationship that don't involve sex: hugging, cuddling, kissing, holding hands, taking quiet walks, etc.

8 Ways to Protect Your Teen

1. Be a good role model.

How often have you heard it said that "It's not what you say but what you do that counts"? By demonstrating love and respect in your own intimate relationship, you'll help your teen to know what behavior should be expected. If you're a single/divorced parent who's dating, you'll also want to be mindful of the message about romantic relationships you want to convey through your behavior.

2. Supervise, supervise, supervise.

There is no substitute for adequate supervision. When your teen was an infant, you wouldn't let her out of your sight in a busy mall. Now that she's a teen, she still needs supervision. More than one pregnant teen or teen parent has told me that if their parents or another adult had been there when they got home from school they probably wouldn't have become pregnant. Of course, many parents work during the afternoons and can't be home. Some suggestions to help protect your teen include enrolling him/her in after-school programs, encouraging participation in extracurricular sports or other activities, and arranging for a grandparent or other adult relative to be home for after-school hours.

3. Set firm curfew limits.

Can you believe that teens actually want limits? It's been said that the teen's job is to push the limits and the parents' job is to set them. If teens don't have firm limits and guidelines they can end up feeling confused. I have had teen patients tell me, "My parents are way too lenient. They let me stay out all night with my friends." These teens seem to be saying, "Don't they care about what could happen to me?" Setting limits is a way of demonstrating caring and concern. Even when they fight them, they need them—desperately. Suggestions for curfew times for different age groups are discussed in Chapter 2.

4. Set clear dating guidelines.

As noted in Chapter 2, teens 14 and younger have the highest risk of experiencing involuntary sex. I believe that teens younger than age 16 are too young to begin one-on-one, unsupervised dating.

And if your teen's partner is three or more years older, the relationship is more likely to involve sex. For example, a 15-year-old girl going steady with a 19-year-old boy has a greater chance of developing a relationship that includes sex than a 15-year-old teen girl going steady with a 16-year-old boy.

5. Help teens stay busy and productive.

This one is very straightforward. If your teen is busy with sports, music, hobbies, or other extracurricular activities, there won't be much time to be involved in sexual activity. If your teen is having a difficult time finding a passion or a particular area of interest, look for volunteer activities. Spending time helping others will promote character and responsibility as well as keep him/her busy.

6. Know what's going on in your teen's world.

While it may be difficult to keep up with the latest teen slang or to become nearly as adept at texting as your teen, you can keep informed about important trends and updates, especially as they relate to teen health. If you're a parent who doesn't keep abreast of the news, you may not know about the vaccine for protection against HPV. Or you might not realize that STD rates among teens have reached epidemic proportions. Informed parents are better prepared to help protect their teens.

7. Keep talking.

Parents often mistakenly assume that once they've made their point about an issue, they don't need to revisit it. Wrong. Teens do not have adult brains. Scientific research shows that the teen brain is only about 80% developed. The last section of the brain to mature is the part that governs reasoning, planning, and judgment. This is one reason you can't assume that because you had that really productive conversation with your teen about the risks of oral sex two months ago that you can cross it off your to-do list forever. Six months later when she says she's "fallen madly in love," she likely needs to revisit the issue and have another conversation about sex.

Likewise, if your teen is on the birth control pill and you've talked to her about the importance of taking the pill reliably, continue to remind her of how important this is. If she's going to a slumber party or away for the weekend with a group of girlfriends, does she have her pills? These are situations when reminders can be especially helpful.

8. Take your teen to a health care provider specifically for a discussion about sexual health.

Introducing young teens to a health care provider who can care for their sexual health needs will allow them to develop a trusting relationship that will make it easier for them to seek sensitive care as they get older.

I want to be clear about the importance of taking your teen to the doctor or other provider specifically for this purpose. According to a CDC study, most high school students did not receive information about preventing STDs or pregnancy when they went in for routine physical exams. Health care providers must make a concerted effort to address sexual health issues with teens. As a busy ob/gyn, I understand why practitioners, who often must see several patients in an hour, might overlook this important issue. Parents should make specific appointments for their child to receive sexual health counseling. In other words, don't say to the health care provider during a visit for a routine school physical or other medical problem, "Oh, by the way, would you talk to my daughter/son about sexual health today?" In this case, teens are likely to receive a much more abbreviated response than they deserve.

You have many options to choose from in terms of health care providers. Some health care providers specialize in the care of teens. Whether you choose a doctor, midlevel nurse, or physician assistant, you'll want to look for the following characteristics:

- Strong interest in teen health care

- Patient and warm manner

- Willing to write directions down and dispense patient education pamphlets

- Encourages patients to call with questions

Successful Communication with Your Teen

The advice in this chapter is presented to make the journey that you and your teen will travel a bit easier. If you keep even a few hints in mind, you will have accomplished much.

Of all the recommendations, I feel that the most important is to demonstrate love and concern to your teen as much as possible. Parents should not only seek to communicate this in their actions but also to verbalize it. Teens who feel nurtured, supported, and loved are more likely to seek your guidance, follow your advice, and avoid risky behaviors.

Telling your children they are loved doesn't mean that their life will be perfect or that they won't make mistakes and sometimes disappoint you, but it will help them to feel supported and better able to make responsible and healthy choices.

Chapter 6

Abstinence: There's More to Discuss Than Saying 'No' to Sex

Many parents are afraid that talking about sex with their teenagers will be taken as permission for the teen to have sex.

—Benjamin Spock

If you've dreaded talking with your teens about why it makes sense to delay having sex, take heart that talking to teens about sex does not encourage it. After all, sex is natural, normal, and enjoyable, and we want to take a positive and healthy approach in our conversations with our children. This chapter explains why "delaying" sex communicates a clearer message to teens than "abstinence," where the hotly debated school sex education controversy is headed, and how to frame the discussion so your values and expectations are clear.

Contrary to what is standard in most texts and articles, I urge parents to avoid using the term "abstinence" when discussing sex with their children. The word abstinence is cumbersome and confusing. How many 13-year-olds can even accurately define what it means? In my own experience, most of them had absolutely no clue what "abstinence" meant. During a recent conversation, a 15-year-old patient had difficulty even pronouncing the word.

Instead of discussing abstinence with your child, why not use simple words that convey exactly what you mean? You don't use medical terms in everyday conversations, so why use them in discussions with teens about sex? When we want our kids to get washed up, we say, "Go get cleaned up," not "Go in the bathroom and exercise good hygiene." We say "Be careful," not "Ambulate carefully." If we refer to a daughter's menstrual period, most of us would simply say "period" or "monthly cycle," rather than "menstruation."

As parents, we want our children to grow up and to have mature and sexually fulfilling relationships. With teens, the issue is about delaying sex until an appropriate time and relationship. In this regard, parents want to be clear when communicating with their kids. If you feel that young people should delay having sex until they are married, be specific about this in your conversations and tell your teen why this is your belief. Perhaps your view is that teens should refrain from sex until they are mature. The definition of maturity will vary, but if for you it's age 18, when young people are eligible to serve in the military and vote, then communicate this to your tween/teen and why you feel this way.

The key here is to convey your values and principles about sex behavior to your child with language that is simple and very clear.

Probing Questions for Parents

As you know from Chapter 2, more than six in 10 high school seniors report having had sex and the vast majority of these teens are unmarried. Your personal philosophy about sex, in relation to age and marital status, will significantly impact how you guide your child.

Unlike the use of alcohol, which is legal at age 21, or obtaining a driver's license, which is usually legal between the ages of 15 to 16, we don't look to the law to tell teens or adults that they are now "ready" for sexual relationships. In guiding their teens, parents must rely on their personal values and morals in addition to their concerns about teen health and safety. Here are some questions to consider as you think through this issue that will help you to clarify and solidify your values:

- At what age did I begin having sex? Would I be OK if my teen were to start at the same age?

- How long, or until what age, should teens delay having sex?

- Did I wait until marriage to have sex?

- Do I expect my teen to wait until marriage to have sex?

- What does my religion teach about sex and marriage? Does my teen share my religious beliefs?

- Do I feel any conflict between what my religion teaches about sex and marriage and what I personally feel is acceptable?

- What would bother me more; my teen having sex without being married or having sex without using protection?

- Which of these issues is most important to me; protecting my teen from pregnancy and STDs or prohibiting my teen from having sex?

Realities About Sex and Abstinence Among Youth

While current sex behavior trends should not be used to counsel our own teens about what behavior is acceptable, it is helpful to know what these trends are. Let's take a look at trends and statistics regarding teen sex behavior:

- Young people today are more likely to delay marriage, not sex.

- By the age of 20, 75% of young people have had premarital sex.

- Of Americans who delayed sex until at least age 20, 80% report that they ultimately had premarital sex.

- Young people are now sexually active as singles for more extensive periods of time.

- Teens with more religious parents and friends are more likely to delay sex.

- Studies have shown that the majority of teens taking a "Virginity Pledge" ultimately have sex before marriage.

Parents, you may view this information with varying perspectives. However, none of us lives in a vacuum. To some extent, we all absorb and are affected by the culture that surrounds us. Recognizing this information can help you to understand the societal trends and pressures our teens face as they make decisions about sex, and help you to better formulate your approach to your teen's sex education

Abstinence-Only vs. Comprehensive Sex Ed Debate

While parents are the primary sex educators of their children, the role of the educational system is also important. There is ongoing controversy over how best to educate our children in the classroom when sex is the subject. The debate centers on whether "Abstinence-Only Sex Education" or "Comprehensive Sex Education" is best for our kids.

Let's look at the differences between these two forms of education.

The abstinence-only approach focuses on teaching young people that abstaining from sex until marriage is the best means of ensuring that they avoid unintended pregnancy and infection with HIV and other STDs. It contains an eight-point definition that educators teach to youth. Among these points are the following:

- Has as its exclusive purpose, teaching the social, psychological, and health gains to be realized by abstaining from sexual activity

- Teaches abstinence from sexual activity outside marriage as the expected standard for all school-age children

- Teaches that sexual activity outside of the context of marriage is likely to have harmful psychological and physical effects

These principles are often associated with religious beliefs. Abstinence-only programs in the U.S. may differ from one locale to another, but they generally do not cover STD prevention with condom use and do not give information about birth control.

Comprehensive sex education programs are currently available in some states. Unlike abstinence-only programs, comprehensive programs present abstinence as a choice, although the benefits of abstinence in preventing pregnancy and STDs are generally given strong emphasis. Information about birth control to prevent pregnancy and condom use to prevent STDs is also presented. As one educator states, "Comprehensive sex education programs try to address the needs of all youth who practice the full spectrum of sexual activity—ranging from abstinence until marriage at one end to multiple sexual partners on the other."

The goal of comprehensive sex education is to equip young people to protect themselves from pregnancy and STDs when they do decide to have sex, and to make healthy, well-informed decisions about their sexual behavior. This approach emphasizes that sex education is a human right and that young people should have access to information about topics that affect them and the decisions they make.

Many who support comprehensive sex education argue that our society must deal with the sexual reality that teens face today and the consequences of their sex behavior, as reported from the research. Those who support abstinence-only education argue that our society cannot afford to move away from the ideal of sex within a committed, marital relationship and that the ideals of love and intimacy within marriage are paramount.

Our efforts to understand what type of education is best for America's children should hone in on what research data tell us.

What Does Research Tell Us Ab

- A study of 35 Comprehensive Sex Education programs around the world found there was ***no evidence that comprehensive sex education programs encouraged sexual activity among teens***.

- The same study concluded that abstinence-only programs are less effective than comprehensive programs.

- Teens in countries comparable to the U.S., where comprehensive sex education is taught, have much lower rates of teen pregnancy and STDs.

- A congressionally mandated evaluation of federally funded abstinence-only programs in America found that rates of abstinence and unprotected sex in students who took part in the programs were the same as students who did not take part in the programs.

- The vast majority of parents of junior high school students believe that birth control and other methods of preventing pregnancy are appropriate topics for sex education in schools.

- The vast majority of Americans support comprehensive sex education.

- Most teens and adults think it is somewhat or very important for society to give teens a strong message that they should wait to have sex until they are at least out of high school.

Where Do We Go from Here?

America is moving toward a more comprehensive sex education philosophy in our schools. However, the jury is still out regarding which philosophy or blend of philosophies works best. It is quite possible that subgroups of teens will respond differently to the same approach.

A landmark study found that African-American sixth- and seventh-graders who were taught abstinence-only sex education were less likely to start having sex within the next two years compared to their peers who received more comprehensive sex education. Unlike most abstinence-only programs, this one did not promote abstinence until marriage.

It is helpful to keep in mind that this is only one of several studies and there are many questions that it raises. For instance, would the same results have been seen if the teens were older, perhaps 10th- or 11th-graders?

This study may do little to alter the positions of those in the abstinence-only vs. comprehensive sex education camps. Perhaps most significantly, it should serve as a reminder to everyone concerned with teen sex education that it is important to remain open to learning from what additional science-based information will teach us in the years to come.

I urge all parents to consider the following principles when considering school-based sex education for our children:

- Public health decisions are best based on sound science and medical accuracy.

- American children and teens are readily familiar with sexual innuendo and material in their daily lives through TV, movies, and the Internet. In the absence of medically accurate, meaningful sex education provided by parents, educators, and health care professionals, they will absorb what these sources have to offer— information that is frequently inaccurate, often demeaning, and potentially harmful.

- The major health organizations that care for our children and teens (American Academy of Pediatrics, American College of Obstetricians and Gynecologists, and The Society of Adolescent Medicine) *all support the promotion of abstinence within the context of comprehensive sex education*. These organizations, along with most Americans, understand the benefits of teens delaying sex. However, they do not want information to be withheld from teens.

- Knowledge empowers. It is critical to arm our teens with knowledge that they can use to protect themselves when they choose to engage in sex (whether during their teens years or in adulthood; married, or unmarried).

99

- Morals and values definitely have a place in the sexual education and rearing of children. However, the emphasis for this should be within the family.

- Ultimately, teens must be responsible for their sexual decisions and any negative consequences of those decisions. Parents influence, but do not have the ultimate control over the sexual behavior of their teens.

However, in order for teens to be responsible, they must be properly educated and have full access to sexual health care. Many of the teens I have interviewed who experienced unintended pregnancy made comments such as, "It just happened," or "I never really thought it would happen to me." This type of ignorance can no longer be viewed as an acceptable or "typical teen" response. All teens need to receive ongoing sex education from parents and educators, so they understand the seriousness of their responsibility for the sexual decisions they make.

In reviewing abstinence-only vs. comprehensive sex education philosophies, do keep in mind that the overwhelming majority of Americans want the same outcome. They want children born into loving, nurturing homes where mature adults are present and able to give kids the guidance and support they need. They also understand and support the benefits of teens' delaying sex.

What Helps Teens Delay Sex?

As mentioned earlier, most Americans are in agreement about the benefit of teens' delaying sex. Let's take a look at issues that specifically affect teens' decisions to delay sex.

1. Fear of pregnancy and STDs

    As noted in Chapters 3 and 4, teen pregnancy and STDs are immense problems for teens, their families, and our society at large. Birth control measures and condom use notwithstanding, many teens just don't feel sex is worth the risk. As one teen remarked to me, "I just wouldn't want to chance that I'd be that one-in-one-hundred person who got pregnant while using birth control."

2. Religious beliefs

    According to The National Campaign to Prevent Teen Pregnancy, religious faith and a strong moral sense are very important in teens' decisions regarding abstinence. And, in their surveys, the majority of teens and adults express that they want more involvement from churches and other houses of worship in teen pregnancy prevention. This view from teens about the importance of their religious beliefs was echoed by many of the teens I interacted with during seminars. And, other teens like Daniela, a 20-year old interviewed for a notable *Newsweek* article on virginity, stated that her decision to be abstinent came from strong family values and deep spiritual convictions.

    Most faith traditions promote the avoidance of sex outside of marriage. And, while those who adhere to the faith may not always adhere to this sex guideline, studies show that teens from religious families and those whose friends regularly attend religious services are more likely to delay sex until age 18 or later compared to teens who don't have these religious influences.

3. Exposure to someone who's suffered negative consequences of early sex

    Sometimes, teens are persuaded to delay sex because someone they know didn't and either got pregnant or contracted an STD. The highlight of the Teen Pregnancy and STD Prevention Seminars I chaired was usually the guest speaker—a teen or former teen who had engaged in early, unprotected sex and suffered the consequences. Their stories were frequently heart-wrenching as they described how their lives were forever changed because of their choices. Their messages were powerful to the other teens.

4. Knowledge that the consequences of teen pregnancy would interfere with their goals

   This was voiced by LaToya, an 18-year-old profiled in the *Newsweek* article, who plans to remain a virgin until marriage. She states, "My career choices are going to need a lot of time and effort." Her goal is to graduate from college and get a job; she wants to stay focused and independent.

5. Sense of their own unreadiness

   This sentiment was voiced by Alice, also interviewed for the *Newsweek* article. Although 18 years old, she felt that she wasn't mature enough to handle the deep intimacy exposed in a sexual relationship.

   Lucian, an 18-year-old male, decided to become a secondary virgin after experiencing an unsatisfactory first sex that lacked emotional intimacy. He stated, "I'm looking forward to an intimate experience with my wife, who I'll truly love and want to spend the rest of my life with. It's kind of corny, but it's for real."

6. They haven't met the right person

   For many teens, it's a less complicated matter. If they're not romantically interested in someone, then sex is just not that big an issue. During the seminars I led, teens ranked "feeling in love" as the most important influence in deciding whether they would have sex. The truth of the matter is that most teens are not interested in having random sex. According to The National Campaign to Prevent Teen Pregnancy, 85% of teens surveyed support the notion that sex should only take place in committed relationships.

Reasons Why Teens Do Not Delay Having Sex

Just as there are many reasons that teens delay having sex, there are several factors that make it less likely they will delay having sex. Many of these have been reviewed earlier, especially in Chapter 2. This section will reemphasize these reasons and introduce additional risks.

1. Peer or partner pressure

    These social pressures will forever be a part of the teenage experience. Partner pressure appears to be more significant than peer pressure.

2. Sex in the media

    The sexual content in media, especially on TV and in the movies, continues to increase. Studies confirm that the high sex content in media is associated with earlier sex and higher risks for teen pregnancy.

3. Lack of adult supervision

    It seems like such an obvious factor, so why is lack of adult supervision for teens such a commonplace issue? Most parents work, whether they reside in two-parent or single-parent households. This fact provides a key ingredient that is needed for teens to have sex— opportunity. This came through loud and clear from many of the previously pregnant teens who spoke at our seminars. One teen remarked in very distinct terms, "If my mom had been there when I got home from school, I would have never had sex."

4. Boredom

    Are you surprised? Leo Tolstoy puts this in perspective,

    "Boredom: the desire for desires."

The truth is that when teens have little in the way of constructive activities to spend their time, they're more at risk for becoming sexually active. One 17-year-old-teen stated, "If towns had more things to do and places to go for teens, then I am sure that the sexual activity rates would go down."

5. Alcohol/drugs

    As you know, the use of alcohol and drugs by teens is not only illegal, but significantly increases the likelihood that they will engage in early, unintended, and unprotected sex.

6. Family dynamics

    Those family factors that are associated with early sex include: being born to teen parents, having an older sibling who had sex at an early age, and having divorced parents.

What Can You Do to Help Your Teens Delay Sex?

In this chapter, we've reviewed topics ranging from the values that we, as parents, must clarify before we can guide children about sex to what sex education programs in schools are most effective, to what motivates teens to delay or not delay having sex. In the final analysis, you remain the primary sex educators of your children and you must never underestimate the power you have to influence your children.

What more, specifically, can you do to help your teens understand the benefits of delaying sex?

Top 10 Measures You Can Take to Help Teens Delay Having Sex

1. Embrace activities which have been shown to help teens delay having sex, such as sports and volunteer work.

2. Remind teens that they have only six years to be a teen (ages 13 to 19). These years are meant to be a time for growing up, having fun, hanging out with friends, and concentrating on school so they can pursue higher education or enter the work force. They shouldn't have to spend their teen years worrying about protecting themselves against pregnancy or STDs.

3. Avoid using abstinence or other technical terms when talking to your teens about sex. Instead, use simple words that describe exactly what you mean. An example would be, "I know it seems like everyone your age is having sex, but I believe it's important for you to wait until you're older and more mature."

4. Focus on being that sensitive, open-minded, and nonjudgmental parent who gives clear expectations to children.

5. Make sure that your teen understands that there are many age-appropriate ways to express affection with their romantic partners and that they don't have to engage in vaginal, oral, or anal sex to be intimate with another person. However, don't underestimate the intensity of romantic feelings that teens may experience.

6. Do recognize that teens who are connected spiritually and who express religious beliefs are more likely to delay having sex. If your faith and religious beliefs are important to you, talk with your teen about why these beliefs matter to you, and what they have added to your

life. However, do not assume that a more religious teen is not at risk for unprotected sex, pregnancy, or STDs.

7. Continue to guide your teen and promote positive messages even when it seems your teen isn't listening. After all, aren't the teen years supposed to be rebellious years? Sometimes teens will take some, but not all, of your advice.

    For example, you strongly encouraged your teen to delay sexual activity until adulthood and/or marriage, but find out that she has chosen to do otherwise. Perhaps because of your guidance, she waited until age 17 vs. age 14 to enter into a sexual relationship and used birth control, or had one sex partner and not multiple sex partners. You may not have had the exact effect that you wanted, but you made a difference.

8. Search for community seminars or events promoting teen sexual health that you can attend with your preteen/teen. These can provide valuable information and stimulate positive conversations about values, sex, and consequences.

9. Remind your teen of the importance of delaying sex in preventing pregnancy and STDs. However, stress the importance of protection for teens who do choose to have sex and don't worry about sending a "mixed message".

    There are numerous situations in which people comfortably hold what are considered to be conflicting points of view. For example, many Americans oppose war, but they squarely support adequately arming the troops who must fight the war. Another example is that most Americans believe that marriage should last forever; however, they surely recognize divorce as a viable and often necessary option.

On this point, give your teen the most clear and honest message possible. Your honesty and concern will come through and that will speak volumes.

10. Remember that you are the anchor and moral authority for your children. Educators have an important role in sex education, and the health care system is critical in providing sexual health information and medical care. Ultimately however, it is what you say and do throughout your child's teen years that will have the greatest impact.

Chapter 7

Contraception for Teens: Myths, Unique Needs, and More

We want far better reasons for having children than not knowing how to prevent them.

—Dora Winifred Black Russell

In an ideal world, teens would always obey, never rebel or push the limits, and if their parents discouraged or forbade them to have sex, they wouldn't. In that world, every teen's room would be neat, the trash would disappear as if by magic and without your ever having to ask to have it taken out, and there would be a zero rate of teen pregnancy. We know better.

Perhaps you're a parent who feels uncomfortable about birth control education for your teen. I've talked with many parents who worry that educating teens about birth control is like saying, "Go ahead and have sex." It isn't, and I ask parents who have this concern to consider this example:

You've made it clear to your teen in no uncertain terms that underage drinking is unacceptable, and you've talked to him or her about the risks associated with teen alcohol use. However, if your teen went to a party and ended up drinking, would you be relieved to know that your message about the risks of drinking and driving had sunk in, and that he or she knew better than to get behind the wheel and called you for a ride instead?

If you were relieved that your teen wouldn't drink and drive, you should also be relieved to know that your teen's knowledge about birth control and the risks of unprotected sex greatly lowers the likelihood that he or she will have unprotected sex. Educating your teen about birth control doesn't mean you think teen sex is acceptable. The education allows teens to be more responsible if having sex is a choice they make, and 70% of them make that choice by the time they leave the teen years. ***That's why it's so important that teens be educated about birth control before they are in a sexually intimate situation.*** In this chapter, I'm going to shed light on prevailing myths about teens and birth control, review optimal birth control methods for teens, and explain why teens often don't use birth control or use it incorrectly.

Abstinence. Birth control education. With teens and sex, the two don't necessarily conflict, despite what some parents believe. There is **no evidence** that talking to or educating teens about birth control leads to an increase in sexual activity. I also want to assure you that you can choose the level of detail about birth control you share with your teen. You may decide to share the full explanation you'll find here, or talk in more general terms about birth control and then take your teen to a health care provider for a discussion of teen sexual health.

As discussed in Chapter 3, teen pregnancy is a major problem in the U.S., with teen pregnancy rates that surpass those in many comparable, industrialized countries. This is unacceptable! In countries with lower teen pregnancy rates, teens often have more education about and access to birth control. Parents, we can and we must do better.

TOP BIRTH CONTROL MYTHS AMONG TEENS

Teen immaturity and lack of knowledge may lead teens to try to avoid pregnancy with what they think is "birth control," but what may actually be a combination of myth and superstition and, thus, doomed to fail. These myths demonstrate misunderstanding of this basic reproductive fact:

Any act that causes semen (which contains sperm) from a boy's penis to come into close contact with a girl's vaginal area can lead to pregnancy.

These are common myths that your teen may falsely believe:

Myth #1: You can't get pregnant the first time you have sex.

Fact: There's no such thing as a pass for beginners. If a girl happens to have unprotected sex near the time her egg is released from the ovary (ovulation), she can very easily become pregnant. A girl can become pregnant for a few days before, during, and after she ovulates (releases an egg from her ovary).

Myth #2: Pregnancy won't occur if the male partner "pulls out" or "withdraws" before he comes (has an orgasm).

Fact: Withdrawal is not a highly effective method of birth control, but is used by up to 10% of teens. Failure rates of up to 27% have been reported. For one thing, withdrawal requires a certain amount of self-control during the sex act which might be difficult for most teen males. And, before a male partner comes, he releases pre-ejaculation fluid into the vagina and this fluid may contain sperm.

Myth #3: You can't get pregnant if both partners are standing up.

Fact: If the rationale behind this one is that the sperm will travel the wrong direction, down the vagina instead of up—wrong. Sperm can be compared to torpedoes and the egg to their target. Gravity will ***not*** keep sperm from reaching the egg.

Myth #4: A girl won't get pregnant if she has sex during her period.

Fact: Makes sense, right? It's easy to understand why this myth would be believed, and the fact is that it's unlikely for a girl to become pregnant while she's on her period. Generally speaking, ovulation (when the egg is released from the ovary and pregnancy becomes possible) occurs about two weeks prior to the start of a period. However, in some cases bleeding may occur without ovulation. If a girl has sex during this bleeding and ovulates soon afterward, she could potentially get pregnant since sperm can live in her body for several days.

Myth #5: Douching (rinsing the vagina) after sex will prevent pregnancy.

Fact: This one is kind of hard to even imagine. OK, on your mark, get set, go—mad dash to the bathroom after sex, douching gear in hand, racing to rinse the vagina. It just won't work. Why? Because **sperm** are very determined to reach their target, the egg. They travel very fast and can reach the egg *in a matter of minutes*. No amount of racing to rinse the sperm out of the vagina will work—sorry.

Myth #6: Pregnancy won't occur if sex takes place in water.

Fact: Such an array of choices—Jacuzzi tubs, swimming pools, fresh water ponds, etc. However, teens who think that having sex while submerged in water is a form of birth control will only get into a lot more "hot water" than they realize. There is just no evidence to support that having sex in water will prevent pregnancy.

Myth #7: Two condoms are better than one

Fact: Condoms are used by a majority of teens. Information on their benefits and limitations will be discussed later in this chapter. A teen might think that two condoms will offer better birth control protection. This isn't true. When one condom is placed over another, damage to the material can occur and increase the risk of failure.

Myth #8: No method of birth control is 100% effective.

Fact: Abstinence is a form of birth control and is the only method that is 100% safe and effective in preventing pregnancy.

The prevalence of these myths underscores one of the reasons why sex education for teens is so important. Some teens may be very mature but many are still very naïve about birth control. And while they may think they "know it all" as Arnold H. Glasglow asserts when he says, "Telling a teenager the facts of life is like giving a fish a bath," the truth is they need a lot of education and support. In order to give guidance on this topic, you need to have a firm, working knowledge of birth control issues and methods.

Test Your Knowledge

Take this short quiz to see how well you understand current statistics on teens, birth control use, and pregnancy.

1. What percentage of teen pregnancies occurs within the **first month** of the initiation of sex?

     a. 5%

     b. 20%

     c. 50%

2. What percentage of teen pregnancies occurs within the **first six months** of the initiation of sex?

     a. 10%

     b. 25%

     c. 50%

3. What percentage of teens reports using birth control during their **first sexual intercourse**?

     a. 30%

     b. 50%

     c. 75%

Answers: (1-b, 2-c, 3-c)

The point here is that teen pregnancy is very likely to occur within the first several months after a teen has sex for the first time. And, teens face extremely high odds of becoming pregnant within a year if they do not use birth control. When they do use birth control, they are more apt to use it incorrectly or inconsistently. I wish I had a dollar for every time a pregnant teen patient told me she "just forgot" to take her birth control pills.

Birth control options that are most suitable for teens are presented next.

Abstinence

No conversation on birth control for teens would be complete without a reminder about the importance of abstinence, covered in depth in Chapter 6. The methods described below allow sex to be safer, but none is 100% safe or as effective as abstinence.

Best Birth Control Options for Teens

There is a dizzying array of birth control choices, both prescription and over the counter. I will review several key methods for teens in detail and discuss what makes them teen-friendly.

- Condoms

- The birth control pill

- The birth control shot

- The implant placed in the arm

- The intrauterine device (IUD)

- The vaginal ring

- The birth control patch

Male Condoms: What They Can and Can't Do

Adults often think condom use can solve the problem of teen pregnancy. Not true. Condom use is very important for sexually active teens, but it doesn't offer the best protection against pregnancy because of its failure rate of about 15%.

The critically important role of condoms is to protect teens against STDs and as a backup method for pregnancy prevention. For example, if a teen girl uses a primary method of birth control such as the pill or the shot, the condoms serve as extra protection in case the pill is forgotten or the shot isn't given on time. Likewise, if the condom breaks or is used incorrectly, having the other form of birth control in use helps guarantee against pregnancy. **Using a condom with another birth control method is called "dual contraception" and it's a concept that can go a long way in helping to reduce teen pregnancy.**

The condom (rubber) is the most commonly used method to prevent pregnancy in teens. According to a CDC survey, the majority of sexually active teens reported using a condom at their last sexual encounter.

We can't be falsely reassured by reported rates of condom use among teens, however, because they often use condoms incorrectly, inconsistently, or both.

Teens and Condoms	
Advantages	Disadvantages
• Protects against HIV and other STDs (most important) • No prescription required • Affordable/available in most drug and grocery stores • Generally safe, with rare side effects • Generally easy to use • Allows male partners to participate in pregnancy prevention	• Higher failure rate—15% the first year • Some males report less enjoyment with sex • Requires a mature, responsible attitude • Some teens are uncomfortable purchasing condoms • Not all teens are familiar with correct condom use, which can contribute to an increased failure rate

In my experience with teens, condoms also have other limitations. Very often, teen sexual activity is unplanned and the couple doesn't have a condom when they need it. Teens are more likely than adults to act on impulse. They just don't think like adults who may have their

Viagra or Cialis on hand, always "being ready for the moment." And, some teens report their belief that using a condom would mean that sex was planned. This attitude is very real, and reflects the conflicted feeling many teens have about sex.

Some teens stop using condoms when their relationship becomes long term. They follow advice they've heard or read that suggests that if the relationship is long-term, monogamous (no cheating), and if both partners have tested negative for HIV and other STDs, that it's safe to stop using condoms. They believe it's OK if the girl just takes her birth control pill or uses whatever other method she's chosen. I would advise against this as teen relationships are much more likely to be on-again, off-again and because sexually active teens may have multiple partners.

If your teen is going to use condoms, what can you do to help insure that this method is used correctly? Don't worry—I know that most parents cringe with embarrassment at the thought of trying to teach their teen how to use a condom. You don't have to do this yourself! You may decide to have your teen learn about condom care and use at sex education classes, from a doctor or other health care provider, or even through Web-based instruction (see Chapter 10). Condoms will be discussed further when we review STD prevention in Chapter 8.

The Birth Control Pill

The birth control pill has been used by more teen girls than any other hormonal method, despite the fact that it is not the most effective method of birth control. A detailed discussion of the birth control pill will be presented.

There are two types of birth control pills available. ***Combination*** birth control pills are standard and contain two hormones, estrogen and progestin. ***Progestin-only*** pills contain one hormone, progestin, and are often referred to as the ***minipill***. The minipill is frequently prescribed for teen girls or women who have a medical condition, such as high blood pressure or migraine headaches, that makes taking the estrogen in the combination pill less safe.

How do birth control pills work? Combination birth control pills prevent the ovary from releasing an egg each month (ovulation) so that the sperm has nothing to unite with to begin a pregnancy.

The progestin-only pill also prevents ovulation, but not as consistently as the combination pill. However, the progestin-only pill also thickens the mucus in the cervix and thins the lining of the uterus, or womb. The thicker mucus makes it harder for sperm to travel through the cervix.

You may have heard of the ***extended or continuous use*** of the birth control pill. These types of regimens can allow women to have between zero to four periods a year, instead of a period every month. A health care provider can give your teen detailed information about these options. Specific brands of birth control pills are designed and packaged for extended use; however, any combination pill can be prescribed to be used this way.

Important Considerations About Birth Control Pill Use in Teens

The birth control pill does not provide a panacea for teen girls. However, in my experience the majority of sexually active teens who come in to my office are either already on the pill, have been on the pill in the past, or are seeking to be on the pill. The birth control pill is very familiar and acceptable to teens, easy to use, has minimal side effects, and with correct use is effective 98 to 99% of the time. The phrase "with correct use" is very important here. With typical use, the birth control pill has a failure rate of approximately 8%.

Herein lies the biggest problem with teens and the pill—incorrect or inconsistent use. Because of this, the actual effectiveness of the pill in teens can drop. In speaking with pregnant teens or those who have given birth, the comments I hear about why the pill failed frequently sound like this:

> "I just kind of took the pill on whichever days
> I remembered to."

"I ran out of pills."

"I started having my period early, so I just stopped the pill."

I firmly believe that with adequate counseling, these problems of incorrect or inconsistent birth control pill use in teens can be overcome. A health care provider can talk with your teen about the importance of taking the pill at about the same time each and every day, and evaluate whether she is likely to comply with this method.

Here are benefits of the pill that go beyond preventing pregnancy:

- Reduces severe menstrual cramps, a common reason for missing school

- Regulates menstrual cycles and allows teens to plan around their periods

- Significantly lightens menstrual flow and reduces the likelihood of anemia

- Improves acne, a reason many teens ask for the pill

Let's look at some of the disadvantages of the birth control pill along with helpful solutions to these drawbacks:

Birth Control Pill Drawbacks	*My Solutions/Recommendations*
• Must be taken every day	• Take at the same time daily, preferably in the a.m. and as part of a routine (e.g., after brushing teeth). This reduces the likelihood she'll forget, and is important for effectiveness. If she takes the pill in the a.m. one day and the p.m. the next, it may not be effective. • She can set a cell phone reminder!
• Nausea, breast tenderness, or irregular bleeding may cause a teen to stop taking the pill abruptly	• Encourage your teen to hang in there—side effects usually resolve in 2 to 3 months. • Remind your teen not to stop taking the pill abruptly, but to talk with her doctor about any issues.
• Your teen may forget to take her pill	• Be sure that she's familiar with the instructions in her pill packet that detail what to do if she misses one or more pills. This underscores the importance of dual contraception with condoms.

Now that we've reviewed the advantages of birth control pills for teens, as well as how to manage the disadvantages, let's look at common myths that keep many teens from using the pill.

Myth: The pill makes you fat.

Fact: This myth is the most common complaint I hear from teens. Teens are very image-conscious and it can be difficult to persuade them to use anything that might cause weight gain. Several studies show that birth control pills do not cause weight gain when compared with women taking placebo (pills with no medication in them). In my experience, weight gain for teen patients on the birth control pill has not been a problem. If mild weight gain does occur, switching to another pill with a different hormonal mix may be all that is needed to resolve this.

Myth: The pill causes cancer.

Fact: The birth control pill is actually associated with protection against ovarian and uterine cancer. The association between the pill and the later development of breast cancer is controversial, but there is no conclusive evidence that the pill causes breast cancer.

Myth: After you stop the pill, you won't be able to get pregnant.

Fact: This is untrue. Most women who had normal ovulation and regular periods prior to starting the birth control pill will continue to have regular ovulation and menstrual cycles immediately after stopping the pill and will be able to conceive without difficulty.

Myth: The pill is bad for your body.

Fact: Many studies document the safety and benefits of the birth control pill. No long-term problems have been shown in teens/women who are appropriate candidates for the birth control pill. Women who have a history of blood clots, severe high blood pressure, heart disease, stroke, breast cancer, and liver disease should not take the pill. These conditions are rarely seen in teens.

Emergency Contraception—What Every Parent and Teen Should Know

Emergency contraception (EC) is a form of birth control that every parent and teen should be aware of. Unlike other forms of birth control, emergency contraception is not used continually, but only in emergencies following unprotected or inadequately protected sex. It is also sometimes referred to as the ***morning-after*** or the ***postcoital*** pill.

Emergency contraception is available in different pill forms or as an IUD. A single-dose pill is available over the counter and without a prescription.

Emergency contraception is very effective in preventing pregnancy. The earlier emergency contraception is used, the more effective it is. **Ideally, it is used within three days, but can be effective when used up to five days after unprotected or inadequately protected sex.** The term unprotected sex can mean that no birth control method was used or that a condom was used and broke, or clearly was used incorrectly. Unprotected sex also occurs when a woman forgets to take her birth control pills and has sex.

Emergency contraception works to prevent pregnancy by various mechanisms, depending on the type that is used. Examples include inhibiting or delaying ovulation and interfering with the ability of sperm to reach the egg.

Some parents voice concern that using emergency contraception is like having an abortion. Leading medical organizations like the World Health Organization and the American College of Obstetricians and Gynecologists assert that emergency contraception does not act in this way.

When emergency contraception is used, condoms must be used until the girl's next period, and should continue to be used consistently for protection against STDs. And, any teen who needs emergency contraception should also be counseled about using an effective long-term method of birth control.

Prepared for an Emergency

Your teen can obtain emergency contraception before she needs to use it. This is called ***Advanced Provision***. In using Advanced Provision, health care providers discuss emergency contraception and actually dispense it so that the teen has it should she ever need it. Having emergency contraception on hand has not been shown to increase the incidence of unprotected sex or to decrease regular birth control use in youth.

Teens and Emergency Contraception	
Advantages	Disadvantages
• Helpful for teens who are at high risk of unplanned, unprotected sex • Safe • Available without a prescription (only one pill form) • Does not cause risk to a pregnancy if a teen girl takes it not knowing she is pregnant	• Often causes irregular bleeding • May cause side effects like nausea, headache, vomiting, and breast tenderness. A pill to prevent nausea can be taken with emergency contraception to ease this side effect. • Some fear that emergency contraception causes teens to be cavalier about standard, long-term birth control methods. There is no evidence that this is true.

The Birth Control Shot

The birth control shot contains only one hormone, a type of progestin. After the birth control pill, the shot is the second most commonly prescribed method for teens. It is given in the muscle of the arms every 12 weeks. Like the birth control pill, it prevents ovulation.

I have taken care of many teens who have used or were currently using the shot. The biggest advantage of using the shot is that the teen doesn't have to remember to take a pill every day. Thus, the issue of compliance is greatly simplified, but not eliminated completely. The teen still has to remember to make and to keep her appointments for the shot every 12 weeks. It is highly effective, easy to use, and generally well-accepted by teens.

Teens and the Birth Control Shot	
Advantages	Disadvantages
• Given only 4 times a year, which may increase teen compliance • Highly effective; only a 3% failure rate • Decreases menstrual flow. Menstrual flow often completely stops after several months of use. This is very helpful for teens who have anemia (low blood count). • Reduces risk of PID (pelvic inflammatory disease) • Reduces risk of ovarian and endometrial (uterine) cancer	• Irregular bleeding is common in the first few months • Weight gain. Manufacturer suggests that a 3- to 4-lb. weight gain is likely in the first year, but I have seen teens gain 10 lbs. or more. I advise teens to weigh themselves every 1–2 weeks, exercise, and follow a healthy diet to help reduce this side effect. • Some teens dislike shots • Prescription/supervision by a health care provider required • It may take several months for a girl's period to return after stopping the shot. • Prolonged use (more than 2 years) may lead to bone loss/potential increased fracture risk. Recent studies show the bone loss can be reversed after stopping the shot. Teens who choose the shot need to take extra calcium, get regular weight-bearing exercise, and not smoke. While the FDA recommends that its use be limited to 2 years due to bone loss concerns, the World Health Organization suggests that the benefits of the shot outweigh these safety concerns.

Birth Control Implant

A newer, long-acting, and reversible method of birth control, the implant, was approved by the FDA in 2006. This method consists of a small rod placed under the skin in the arm. Like the birth control shot, it also contains a type of hormone called a progestin. The implant is effective for three years. After three years, it must be removed and a new implant placed if the teen girl wants to continue using this method.

The implant prevents pregnancy in several ways, including thickening the mucus in the cervix, which makes it harder for sperm to enter the uterus (womb), thinning the lining of the uterus, and preventing ovulation.

The wonderful thing about the implant is that once it's inserted, the teen has nothing to think about for three years. That's it—no daily pills to take, no shots every 12 weeks. This is an enormous advantage. Add to this its effectiveness (99%) and simplicity, and the implant gives teens another really great option.

It is one of two methods commonly referred to as LARCs (Long-Acting Reversible Contraceptives) and is highly recommended as a method of birth control for teens.

Teens and the Birth Control Implant	
Advantages	Disadvantages
• Provides birth control for 3 years, which makes it an excellent choice for teens • Safe and highly effective, with a failure rate of less than 1%. • Often causes periods to stop, which is highly desirable for some teens • Periods begin again right away when the implant is removed	• Requires a minor surgical procedure to insert—easily done in a physician's office • Causes mild discomfort after it is inserted • Frequently causes irregular bleeding • Sometimes associated with other side effects—weight gain, headaches, breast tenderness, and acne • Associated with mood changes more commonly in teens than in adults

IUD

The intrauterine device (IUD) is also a LARC method and is considered an excellent option for teens because it is highly effective and well tolerated. It is shaped like a T, made of a flexible material and inserted into the uterus by a health care provider. There are several different IUDs available on the market in the U.S. They contain a progestin hormone or copper and provide birth control from three to 10 years (minimum) depending on which type is chosen.

IUDs work in a number of different ways, depending on the type. Their mechanisms of action include, but are not limited to, destructions of sperm, reduction in sperm movement, thinning of the lining of the uterus, and thickening of the cervical mucus.

Is the IUD a good option for teens? Yes. As mentioned previously, it is a highly effective LARC method with a failure rate of less than

1%. The progestin-containing IUD also significantly reduces blood loss with periods. Once the IUD is inserted, your teen won't have to think about birth control for at least three to 10 years, depending on which IUD is chosen.

In the past, there were concerns about the possible increased risk of pelvic infections in teens using IUDs because teens have higher rates of certain STDs. This led to low usage of this method by health care providers. However, studies have shown that the IUD is a safe method of birth control for adolescents. Health care providers are recommending them and the increased use of IUDs in teens is supported by ACOG.

Drawbacks of the IUD include:

- Requires a minor procedure to be inserted

- Causes some cramping and discomfort when inserted

- May be expelled (fall out of the uterus)—uncommon

- May perforate (tear through) the uterine wall— uncommon

- May increase menstrual cramping and blood loss (copper IUD)

Vaginal Ring and The Patch

The vaginal ring and the patch both contain the hormones estrogen and progestin, which are also used in the standard combination pills. Both work like the pill to prevent pregnancy by stopping ovulation, are very effective, and generally share the same overall benefits and drawbacks. They both have reported failure rates of about 8%.

The vaginal ring is a soft, flexible ring which is inserted directly into the vagina. With typical dosing, it is left in place for three weeks and then removed for one week in which the period occurs. One advantage of the ring is that it contains very low levels of hormones.

However, it hasn't been extensively studied in teens and requires a highly motivated teen who is comfortable inserting and removing the ring from her vagina.

The patch is a small, square adhesive that is placed on and sticks directly to the skin. The typical dosing requires that it be changed every week for three weeks and then be removed for one week which allows the period to occur. Studies show that teens using the patch are extremely or somewhat satisfied. One potential problem is that the patch can fall off, completely or partially, which renders it ineffective. And, teens using the patch are exposed to higher levels of estrogen than in other hormonal methods which could place them at higher risk for cardiovascular complications such as blood clots, although studies have not shown this to be a problem.

Teens and Birth Control Failure

We've discussed inconsistent and/or incorrect use as a common reason birth control fails and pregnancy results in teens. There was no condom when your teen needed it. The condom broke or was not placed correctly. Your teen daughter forgot to take her birth control pills or to refill her prescription for the vaginal ring. These are examples of situations that can lead to birth control failure and pregnancy.

One measure parents can take to help prevent birth control failure in teens is to encourage the use of LARCSs (Long-Acting Reversible Contraceptives). These methods, the implant and the IUD, don't require as much effort on the part of teens once they are inserted, are less likely to be discontinued, and are the most effective birth control options.

Some hormonal methods of birth control may be less effective in significantly overweight teens. If applicable, teens should discuss this potential problem with their health care provider.

Many health care providers begin birth control on the same day as the teen's office visit, after appropriate counseling. This approach is called "quick start." Starting the birth control method right away decreases the likelihood that a teen girl won't ever start it, and the quick-start approach has been found to increase the likelihood that she will continue her birth control. Your daughter's health care provider will take extra precautions with this approach, including verifying that your daughter is not pregnant and ensuring back-up control is used, if deemed appropriate.

I talked about the importance of dual contraception, using a condom with another form of birth control. Let me also take a moment to reiterate that teen relationships can frequently be short-lived, or on-again, off-again. Teen girls using birth control, especially shorter-acting methods, often stop their contraception when their relationship breaks up. I counsel teen patients that it's okay to continue using birth control even after they've ended a relationship. That's because I've witnessed cases where a teen girl goes through a breakup and stops taking birth control. She then gets back together with her boyfriend unexpectedly or begins another relationship and becomes pregnant, sometimes after having unprotected sex only once. *The end of a relationship doesn't mean an immediate end to the need for birth control, especially for teens.*

It is extremely important that teens receive thorough and sensitive counseling about birth control from their health care provider to help prevent failure. I strongly urge parents to seek out a provider who has a particular interest in teen sexual health care and who is willing to go the extra mile to help protect your child.

What Keeps Teens from Using Birth Control?

Why don't more teens use birth control? The answer is that significant barriers stand in the way:

- Embarrassment

- False sense of invincibility (It won't happen to me)

- Not knowing where to go to obtain birth control

- Cost

- Fear about confidentiality and that their parents will be informed

Embarrassment

Some teens report being embarrassed to discuss contraception with their health care provider when a parent is present in the examining room. In addition to feeling uncomfortable asking about contraception with their parent in the room, some teens say they are reluctant to discuss birth control with their partner.

I have two recommendations about teen embarrassment and contraception:

1. Allow your teen to have some time alone with the physician. As a parent myself, I fully understand the desire to monitor your teen's care. But as a physician, I also know that a sensitive conversation can be easier to conduct when teens are given a measure of privacy. As a matter of routine, I let parents know that I need a little time alone with their teen during office visits.

2. If you sense that your teen would be unwilling to talk about birth control with a partner, this is an opportunity to discuss readiness for sex. Teens who aren't able to bring up birth control with a partner are not likely to be emotionally ready for a sexual relationship.

False Sense of Invincibility

Many teens just do not perceive themselves as someone who can become pregnant, even when they are having sex. You've probably heard of teens' false sense of invincibility. This explains why teens sometimes do reckless things like illegally racing cars, experimenting with drugs, and yes, having unprotected sex.

It's more than just a notion with teen girls and sex. I stopped being perplexed and really starting understanding the teen mind when pregnant teen after pregnant teen remarked that she "just didn't think it would happen to me," or "I just kind of never really thought about becoming pregnant as a real possibility," or "We just never thought about using birth control." These responses serve to remind us that teens' capacity to truly consider the consequences for certain actions, like unprotected sex, is different from adults. This capacity won't fully develop until adulthood, as pointed out in this anonymous saying: "There is nothing wrong with today's teenagers that 20 years won't cure."

Not Knowing Where to Go

Many teens who are covered by their parents' insurance can obtain birth control through their doctor or health care group. These teens would generally not have a problem knowing where to get birth control, but are still often concerned about confidentiality.

The Title X Family Planning Program provides for sexual health care services for teens who are covered by Medicaid. However, many uninsured or low-income teens may not know that these services are available or where to go for care. These teens can usually obtain health care from a provider who accepts Medicaid or at a county hospital or community clinic. Parents who qualify for Medicaid can learn more about Title X in Chapter 10.

Cost

Some insurance plans cover 100% of the cost of birth control, others cover only part of the costs for birth control, and some methods may not be covered at all. Teens covered by their parents' insurance may still have to pay some out-of-pocket costs for birth control. Unless the teen has her own income, she has to rely on her parents or others for the money to pay for birth control.

Teens who are eligible for Medicaid under Title X should have coverage for birth control.

Confidentiality, Privacy

This barrier is perhaps the most complex and the most significant. Lack of confidential care has repeatedly been shown to be a barrier to teens' obtaining sexual health care. Many teens simply won't seek medical services for birth control or STD evaluation and treatment if they can't be sure their parents won't be informed. In one study, 18% of teens surveyed listed fear that their parents would find out as a the primary reason for not using contraception. Another study showed that 47% of sexually active young women indicated that mandatory parental notification (which would require the health care provider to notify the parent about prescribing birth control to their teen) would cause them to stop using family planning services. It is critical for sexually active teens to be able to prevent pregnancy.

In 1988, several major health organizations that promote adolescent health care supported a policy that emphasized the fact that barriers concerning parental involvement should not be allowed to stand in the way of medical care that teens need. In reality, despite laws designed to ensure that teens are provided with confidential services when they seek birth control, there can be pitfalls.

Interestingly, one study found that the availability of confidential health services for teens did not prevent them from discussing their health care visit with their parents. In general, teens would tell their parents if they had a serious health problem. The upshot of this study was that teens want access to confidential sexual health services, but the majority of them are willing to discuss these visits with their parents. This is an important finding, because one of the biggest obstacles to providing confidential sexual health care to teens is the belief, by many parents, that this service undermines the parent-child relationship.

I've witnessed very different parental responses to the issue of teens and confidential sexual health care. I've observed an occasional situation where the parent was anxious about the teen becoming sexually active and was insisting that birth control be prescribed. When I had a few minutes alone with the teen, I learned that the teen didn't want birth control and wasn't planning on becoming sexually active. I've had several teens come to the office with their mothers specifically for the purpose of obtaining birth control. In these situations I am reassured by the open communication between the parent and the teen. At the opposite end is the parent who firmly maintains that her daughter is not interested in having sex and doesn't need birth control information. Sometimes, I've heard this from parents, then learned something different after talking to their teen, which tells me there is a disconnect between what the teen is thinking and what the parent understands.

Important Facts About Teens, Privacy, and Contraception

All parents should have some basic information about what the law has to say about teens, sex, and confidential health care.

- Most states have Minor Consent Laws which allow minors, ages 12-17 (age limits can vary by state), to give their consent (permission) for certain medical services. These services include family planning (pregnancy, STD testing and treatment, and birth control).

- In order for states to receive federal funds for family planning services under Title X of the Public Health Services Act, they must offer birth control and other reproductive (sexual health care) to minors on a confidential basis.

- Specific details of Minor Consent Laws vary by state.

- It is important to note that both federal and state laws encourage minors to involve their parents in the health care services they receive and the decisions they make.

As a physician, I encourage open communication between teens and their parents, even as I am providing confidential sexual health care.

It's important to understand what the law has to say about the issue of confidential health care services for teens, but it's even more important for you to zero in on your communication with your teen. Research from the National Campaign to Prevent Teen Pregnancy shows that one in two teens trusts his or her parents most to obtain accurate and complete information about birth control. Only about 12% of teens surveyed said they would trust a friend more than their parents. Teens who can talk with their parents about sex and birth control are more likely to use birth control if they have sex and are less likely to become pregnant. No law or policy can ever trump open parent-teen communication when it comes to ensuring that teens receive the appropriate sexual health services that are so important to their well-being.

Chapter 8

Beyond Vaccines: What Parents Need to Know to Prevent Teen STDs

An ounce of prevention is worth a pound of cure.

—Benjamin Franklin

From the time their children are infants until they reach adulthood, parents view their role as protectors of their children's health and well-being. We use many different sayings to express our concerns:

Look both ways before you cross the street.

Don't play with matches.

Don't open the door for a stranger.

Never get in the car with a driver who's been drinking alcohol or using drugs.

Drive carefully.

We convey these common instructions to our children—all in the hope of keeping them safe from harm.

In Chapter 4, we learned about STDs that affect teens in significant ways—either because they're extremely common and/or because of their potential to cause lifelong complications, even death. In this chapter, the focus shifts to strategic ways that parents and communities can help teens avoid becoming victims of an STD.

Top 8 Common-Sense Measures to Help Prevent Teenage STDs

1. Encourage teens to postpone sex.

   It seems so obvious, and yet how often do teens really get the message that not having sex or at least delaying it until they are much older can save them from the physical and psychological harm that STDs pose? In Chapter 4, we learned that rates of certain STDs like chlamydia and HPV are staggeringly high in our teen population. We also learned that the physical presence of an immature cervix in a teen girl increases her risk of contracting chlamydia or gonorrhea if she is exposed. This information should serve as a red flag warning regarding the tremendous risks teens face from STDs.

   The communication tips in Chapter 5 will help you in guiding your teens to delay sex. And, remember to remind teens of the important goals of the teen years. One dear colleague memorably commented: "*You're only a teenager for a very short time, and in that time your job is to grow up.*" Just think about it—less than one-tenth of an average person's lifespan is spent in the teen years spanning ages 13 to 19. During this brief time, teens should focus on growing up, having fun, and becoming educated so that they can ultimately navigate the very complicated world they will inherit as opposed to engaging in early sex with the associated risks of STDs and pregnancy.

2. Encourage teens to value themselves and to respect their bodies.

   Teens who feel highly valued will be much less likely to succumb to peer pressure to engage in risky sexual behavior. If they do choose to have sex, they will be more likely to protect themselves against STDs by using condoms and using them consistently.

What additional, specific things can parents do to promote this goal?

- Choose and model respectful behavior toward yourself and your own body.

  Do you take time to exercise, eat healthy meals, and keep your weight under control?

  Do you treat yourself with kindness or do you frequently belittle yourself? Are you more apt to take time to pamper yourself with an occasional massage or to bemoan that fact that you have no time for an occasional self-indulgence?

- Give positive strokes to your child.

  How do you feel when someone compliments you? A comment from a coworker as simple as "You look really nice today" can set a positive tone for your entire day. How much more then, do compliments boost the self-esteem and confidence of a child? Statements such as, "I'm so proud of how well you did on your test," "You're such a good friend to all your buddies," or "It's amazing to me how talented you are at writing," are just a few examples that can build your teen's self worth.

- Tell your teen that self-respect includes protecting his or her body.

  Here, I want to mention a risk that many parents and teens may not be aware of.

  STDs have been shown to be transmitted by tattooing and body piercing. Theses art forms have become ever more popular among our youth. The STD most associated with these art forms is hepatitis B.

  HIV has never been shown to be transmitted by tattoos, but medical experts suggest it could be a possibility, and it is an even higher risk with body piercing. It has even been suggested that HPV can be transmitted when a tattoo is received.

Any teen considering a tattoo or a body piercing must be certain that the facility is clean, and that the tattooist or piercer uses sterile gloves, new needles, and new ink (for tattoos). In other words—use caution!

Lastly, I want to mention that a recent study showed that teens who repeatedly cut themselves (a form of self-injury) are more likely to engage in risky sexual behavior and thus are at increased risk of becoming infected with HIV and other STDs. This is because many of these teens share their cutting instruments with others. Teens who participate in this form of self-destruction should be referred for mental health evaluation and made aware of their increased risk for STDs.

3. Support school-based sex education regarding STDs.

    The school environment is ideally suited for educating teens about STDs and for continually reinforcing important prevention measures.

    When I was a teenager, there was no sex education presented at my middle or high school. However, I do vividly remember the drug prevention program. To this day, I can still visualize the video showing a teen, dazed on LSD and about to drive his car off a cliff. This frightening visual worked just as it was supposed to—it scared the living daylights out of me and convinced me that trying a mind-altering drug like LSD was something that I would never want to do.

    Similarly, teens presented with information and visuals showing potentially life-threatening risks associated with certain STDs may be more likely to avoid engaging in risky sexual behavior. Examples include:

- Chlamydia and subsequent PID (pelvic inflammatory disease)—resulting in a tubal pregnancy with massive hemorrhage

- HPV—leading to severe illness from cervical cancer and possibly even death

- HIV—giving rise to physical wasting and death associated with AIDS

Parents, teachers, health care providers, and community leaders are important in guaranteeing that all teens receive accurate information about STDs and their prevention.

4. Help teens to understand the link between substance abuse and STDs.

    Teens who use alcohol and/or drugs prior to having sex are more likely to have unprotected sex and to become victims of sexual assault. Not only can alcohol and/or drug use impair a teen's judgment, it can interfere with the ability of a couple to use a condom correctly.

    Every teens needs to receive this very clear message: **Underage alcohol and/or illegal drug use increases the odds of risky sexual behavior and thus increases the chances of becoming infected with an STD.**

    We live in a celebrity-driven culture where celebrities sometimes make poor choices about drug and alcohol use. Adult role models who choose not to use alcohol or drugs can send powerful and positive messages to our kids about this issue.

5. Promote condom use among teens who choose to have sex.

    Sexual abstinence is the only 100% effective way to prevent STDs. **Outside of abstinence, condom use is the most important way to prevent STDs**. Teens should understand this point just as they understand that brushing their teeth helps to prevent cavities. In addition to recognizing the importance of consistent condom use during sexual activity, teens should also be aware of these points:

- Condom use does not guarantee safe sex. The use of condoms is associated with saf*er* sex. In other words, by using condoms, teens greatly reduce the risk of being infected with an STD, but the risk is not completely eliminated. As pointed out in Chapter 7, condoms can break, slip out, or be used incorrectly by teens.

- Latex condoms are recommended for protection against STDs! If a latex allergy is present, polyurethane condoms offer comparable protection.

- Natural skin condoms (sometimes called lambskin condoms) are not recommended for STD protection.

- Lubricants can be helpful in reducing the risk of a condom tearing. But, the lubricant must be water-based. The use of a contraceptive foam or gel which contains a special ingredient called nonoxynol-9 can also serve as a lubricant. This is highly desired because nonoxynol-9 provides additional protection against HIV.

- Condoms don't last forever! They come with an expiration date—yes, just like a carton of milk. It's important to check the expiration date before a condom is used to make sure that it is still effective.

- Condoms should be available before they're needed. This can be a sticky point for some parents. However, wouldn't you prefer that a condom were available if your teen found himself or herself in an intimate situation that wasn't anticipated?

Having easy access to a condom doesn't increase the likelihood your teen will have sex.

As noted in Chapter 7, it may be difficult for parents to talk to teens about the information provided above and especially about the nitty-gritty details of how to use a condom. Parents can refer their teen to specific websites, such as the one listed in Chapter 10, for the specifics of condom use.

6. Urge STD testing for teens.

How many teens ask the person they're dating if he or she has been tested for HIV before they have sex? My observation is that very few teens think to inquire about any STD testing by their partners. This speaks to one of the many reasons that teenage sexual activity is considered so risky. Teens certainly have the physical ability to perform the sex act, but the emotional maturity needed to think about critical issues before they act may not be fully developed.

Teens and adults alike need to be aware of this information about STD testing:

- The CDC recommends yearly chlamydia testing of all sexually active women under 25 years of age.

- General health guidelines encourage STD testing before any new sexual relationship and for those with or a history of multiple sex partners.

- Teens diagnosed and treated for chlamydia should be retested three months after treatment. This is primarily to screen for reinfection, which is more likely in teens.

- Those diagnosed with certain STDs like chlamydia, gonorrhea, HIV, and syphilis should notify any sex partner they have had within the previous 60 days so that person can seek STD testing and treatment.

There are ample ways to get this information across to teens. Health care providers serve as a front-line defense and should provide teens with this information and monitor them for compliance. Parents can also provide their teens with brochures and websites, such as those listed in Chapter 10, that contain easy-to-read information about STD testing.

In some states, school-based clinics offer HIV and other STD testing. This testing may be provided on school grounds or through referral of students to local health centers or community-based organizations.

7. Promote teen participation in school-based and community STD awareness and prevention programs.

There are several school and community-based programs that provide a host of services aimed at STD prevention. Whether they are sexually active or not, all teens should be knowledgeable about STDs and how best to prevent them. Unfortunately, all too often this is not the case. A recent study showed that only 19% of teen girls were correctly able to identify all nine common STDs as being sexually transmitted. What's more, more than 90% thought that HIV was the only STD with serious consequences. This is simply further evidence of the lack of knowledge about STDs by many teens.

One example of a school-based program is **Safer Choices**. This two-year program, offered to high school students, promotes the concept that choosing not to have sex is the safest choice that teens can make. However, the program also stresses that using condom protection to prevent pregnancy and STDs is a *safer choice,* and that unprotected sex or sex before one is ready is an *unsafe choice.* Safer Choices also includes parents and community members. This program has been found to reduce the number of instances of unprotected sex (no condoms) among teens.

There are many other examples of school- and community-based programs available to teens. Parents and concerned adults do not have to go it alone.

8. Enlist assistance from health care providers.

    Nowhere is the guidance of health care providers more important than in the arena of STD prevention for teens. Health care providers are in an ideal position to warn teens about the dangers of STDs and to offer preventive measures ***before it's too late***.

    It's important for teens to develop a relationship with a health care provider before they become sexually active. By doing so, trust and open communication can be established so that the teen is more likely to seek assistance from that provider about sexual issues when the need arises. As stated in Chapter 7, The American College of Obstetricians and Gynecologists (ACOG) recommends that teen girls visit an obstetrician/gynecologist between ages 13 to 15. It's very important that teen boys also receive sexual health counseling, and this can occur during their annual pediatric care visit.

    I want to emphasize that excellent sexual health care counseling and care can be provided by gynecologists, pediatricians, family practitioners, or midlevel health care providers such as nurse practitioners or physician assistants. What's important here is that you, as parents, let the health care provider know, very specifically, that you want sexual health care to be covered during the visit you are scheduling.

    Here are important points to keep in mind regarding professional preventive STD health care for your teen:

*   Look for a health care provider who communicates a strong interest in adolescent health.

*   Allow your teen private time with the health care provider and understand that your teen has the right to confidentiality about the issues discussed.

- Know that this confidentiality should extend to any questionnaires your teen may need to complete. Let your teen answer any written questions in private.

- Understand that STD testing done on your teen does not confirm that your teen is having sex. Testing may be done for many reasons, including an abundance of caution.

- Help remind your teen to keep any follow-up appointments.

STD Vaccinations: What Parents Need to Know

In this section, we'll review two vaccines available for the prevention of STDs in teens, the HPV vaccine and the hepatitis B vaccine. The majority of the information will be about the HPV vaccine because of its newness and the many concerns that parents express about this vaccine.

The HPV Vaccine

The first HPV vaccine was licensed for use by the Food and Drug Administration (FDA) in 2006. Since then, more than 25 million doses have been distributed in the U.S. In many ways, the advent of this vaccine heralded an exciting new tool in preventing the most common STD in young people. On the other hand, no vaccine in recent history has been associated with so much confusion and worry on the part of parents. What gives?

In my own practice, these are some of the comments from worried parents of my teen patients:

"How can I know that it's been tested thoroughly?"

"It's so new. How can I be sure that there won't be long-term side effects that they don't know about yet?"

"How do I know that it will really work?"

These and other concerns have caused resistance to the use of the HPV vaccine. One recent survey of parents showed that 52% did not plan to vaccinate their daughters within the next year. These anxious parents cited the newness of the vaccine, their lack of information about the vaccine, and a low level of concern about their daughters being at risk for HPV exposure. This same survey noted that parental reluctance about the vaccine was higher for those whose daughters were younger than 13.

Since 2006, three vaccines have been approved by the FDA for the prevention of HPV. The most recently approved vaccine protects against nine types of HPV. I encourage you to consult with your health care provider regarding the specific details about this newest vaccine. The information that follows will help you to make well-informed decisions, based on accurate information, regarding HPV vaccination of your daughters and sons.

- *Why was the HPV vaccine developed?*

   As discussed in chapter 4, HPV is the most common sexually transmitted disease in the U.S. Millions of people are infected with a new HPV infection every year in our country. HPV infections are most common in young people in their late teens and early 20s. It is estimated that the majority of sexually active people will be infected with at least one HPV type in their lifetime.

   Certain strains of HPV are associated with either the development of cervical cancer, precancerous lesions, or genital warts. Over 11,000 new cases of cervical cancer are diagnosed each year in the U.S. and there are more than 4,000 deaths from this disease each year. Worldwide, it is estimated that about 500,000 new cases of cervical cancer are diagnosed each year, and that roughly 240,000 deaths occur from this disease.

This is why the HPV vaccine was developed, to help protect our young people from this extraordinarily common STD and its harmful effects.

- *How does the HPV vaccine work?*

The original vaccine protected against the two HPV types (16 and 18) that cause most cervical cancers and the two types (6 and 11) that cause most cases of genital warts. The newer vaccine protects against five additional HPV types that can cause cancer.

- *Does the HPV vaccine just protect against cervical cancer and genital warts?*

The answer is no, and this is information that is frequently left out of the conversations about the HPV vaccine. It's often referred to as the cervical cancer vaccine.

The HPV vaccine also protects against HPV-associated precancerous lesions, as well as many cancers of the vulva and vagina in females and cancers of the anus in females and males. The HPV vaccine may also reduce the incidence of oropharyngeal (back of the throat) cancers in females and males.

- *What are the specific recommendations for girls receiving the HPV vaccine?*

The CDC recommends that the HPV vaccine be given to girls ages 11 to 12 on a routine basis. It can be given as young as age 9. Girls who do not receive the vaccine at these ages are recommended to receive the same vaccine as a catch-up regimen between the ages of 13 to 26.

- *Should boys and young men receive the vaccine?*

The initial studies on the HPV vaccine were done on girls, and this was followed by the approval of the vaccine for girls. Remember, it is overwhelmingly girls who suffer from the consequences of HPV.

However, it is widely recognized that boys and young men are the primary source of infection for girls and young women, and that they are also at risk for genital warts and cancers of the penis, anus and oropharynx (back of throat). For this and other reasons, in October 2009, an FDA advisory panel approved the HPV vaccine for boys and men between the ages of 9 and 26. ***From 2010 onward, parents of teen girls and boys are encouraged to have their children vaccinated against HPV.***

- *How is the HPV vaccine actually given?*

The vaccine is given as a series of three shots. The shots are usually given in the upper arm. After the first shot, the second shot is given 1-2 months later, and the third shot is given 6 months after the first shot. The series of shots should be completed in six months.

- *How effective is the vaccine?*

It is an extremely effective vaccine and its protection lasts at least eight to 10 years. This interval may be prolonged as additional information is collected.

Currently, there is no recommendation for patients to receive a booster shot to prolong the protection any further.

- *Should my daughter still receive the vaccine if she's already tested positive for HPV?*

Yes. If your daughter tests positive for HPV, it's most likely that she has only one HPV type and she may have a type that is not included in the vaccine. Therefore, she would still be protected against future infection from one of the nine HPV types present in the vaccine. Even if she has been infected with one of the HPV types present in the vaccine, she can still be protected against infection from the remaining HPV types in the vaccine.

- *What side effects are caused by the vaccine?*

  The overwhelming number of side effects are considered nonserious. These include:

  - Pain at the injection site—most common
  - Headaches
  - Nausea
  - Fever
  - Fainting

  A small percentage of serious problems has been reported in girls who received the HPV vaccine; however, it is important to point out that no proof exists that these problems were a direct result of the vaccine. They are reported because the serious problem occurred after the vaccine was given.

- The FDA and the CDC continue to monitor the safety of the HPV vaccine and to support its benefits, effectiveness, and safety.

- *Is the HPV vaccine made from a live virus?*

  No. The vaccine is not made from a live virus. It is made from noninfectious particles. And, it does not contain thimerosal, a mercury-containing preservative that concerns many parents.

- *What other important information should I be aware of?*

  First of all, my biggest bugaboo about the HPV vaccine and teens has to do with follow up. ***Many teens fail to show up for the second and third doses of the vaccine!***

  When teenagers start the vaccine series, it is imperative that they come in as scheduled for the second dose in one to two months and the third dose in six months. Do whatever it takes—mark your calendar in big red letters, send them e-mail reminders, and have the doctor's office call before their next appointment.

If your teen does miss a scheduled shot, it's important to receive the next dose as soon as possible. This should occur even if it's been several months. Talk to your health care provider about questions you may have.

The HPV vaccine is not recommended for pregnant women. If you have a pregnant teen, she should not receive the vaccine during her pregnancy but may receive the vaccine if she's breastfeeding.

In the final analysis, every parent will have to determine what is in the best interest of his or her teen. In the case of the HPV vaccine, I advise strong consideration of what our key governmental health and safety agencies (the FDA and CDC) recommend. Additional information can be obtained by viewing website information in Chapter 10.

Other Proven Ways to Reduce the Risk of Cervical, Vaginal, and Vulvar Cancers

There has been significant emphasis on the HPV vaccine as a preventive measure against cervical cancer, and rightly so. However, there are other important preventive measures in addition to those noted earlier in this chapter. These include:

• *Pap test and HPV screening*

  The Pap test remains the most important test available to screen for cervical cancer. The HPV test is usually done at the same time as the Pap test. What I will say next may seem **contradictory** to many parents. Based on recent American College of Obstetricians and Gynecologists (ACOG) guidelines, neither Pap nor HPV testing is now recommended for teens. As a matter of fact, current guidelines state that testing should be started at age 21 in females. The rationale for these guidelines is based on the knowledge that:

o   When teens become infected with HPV or develop a mildly abnormal Pap test, these findings are very likely to resolve in two to three years and *without treatment*.

o   The risk of cervical cancer is extremely remote in teens (0.1%).

o   Aggressive treatment of HPV and Pap test abnormalities can lead to complications.

Not only have the guidelines for Pap and HPV testing for teens changed dramatically in recent years, they will continue to change as new information is acquired. Some practitioners may still choose to offer Pap and HPV testing to teens. Parents are strongly advised to consult their health care professionals about this issue.

*   *Avoidance of tobacco use*

The use of tobacco has been shown to increase the risk for the development of cervical cancer. Of course, tobacco use is also associated with many other health risks, the most important of which is lung cancer.

*   *Limiting the number of sexual partners*

The more sexual partners that a teen has, the greater the risk for STD infection. While it is ideal for teens to postpone sex, we know that often this does not occur. Parents, educators, health care providers, and others can still help sexually active teens to *reduce their risks further* by stressing the dangers associated with multiple sex partners.

The Hepatitis B Vaccine

As we learned in Chapter 4, hepatitis B infections can be serious and lead to cirrhosis, a chronic illness, or to liver cancer and death. It was also pointed out that sexual transmission is the most common route of spread for hepatitis B in teens.

Fortunately, hepatitis B is a very preventable illness, and vaccination against this infection is by far the most important tool in prevention. Unlike the HPV vaccine, the hepatitis B vaccine has been on the market for many years and its use is not associated with the same kinds of worries surrounding the HPV vaccine. Still, too many teens remain unvaccinated.

Let's take a look at the key points that all parents and teens should know about the hepatitis B vaccine:

- *Every unvaccinated teen should receive the hepatitis B vaccine.*
  At present, the standard recommendation by the CDC is to begin the hepatitis B vaccination series shortly after birth. However many teens have not been vaccinated and they are regarded as a high-risk group. Current recommendations are that "All children and adolescents younger than 19 years of age who have not yet gotten the vaccine should also be vaccinated."
  Many states require that middle school children or seventh-graders complete the hepatitis B vaccine series prior to school entry.
- *There is an alternate schedule of dosing for teens who have not previously received the vaccine.*
  For most individuals, the vaccine is given in three divided doses—initially, at 1 month, and again at 6 months. However, there is a two-dose schedule that is approved for those 11 to 15 years of age. After the initial dose, the second dose is given four to six months later.
- *The hepatitis B vaccine is safe and effective.*
  The first hepatitis B vaccine was approved in 1982. Since then, more than 100 million people have received the vaccine in the U.S. and serious side effects are extremely

rare. A newer vaccine, available since 1986, is currently in use.

This vaccine provides greater than 90% protection against the hepatitis B infection for those who complete the full series of shots.

The vaccine cannot cause a hepatitis B infection. It is made from synthetic materials.

What Other Ways Are Available to Prevent Hepatitis B Infection?

While vaccination is the most effective way to prevent the spread of hepatitis B infections, there are other preventive measures. Remember, while teens are most likely to become infected through sex, the infection can be spread any time that blood, semen, or other body fluids enter the body of someone who is not infected.

Additional preventive measures include:

- Use of condoms with all sex partners

- Avoiding direct contact with blood and bodily fluids

- Cleaning up blood spills with a fresh diluted bleach solution

- Covering all cuts

- Avoiding the sharing of sharp items such as razors, nail clippers, earrings, or body rings and verifying that new, sterile needles are used for ear or body piercing, tattoos, and acupuncture

- Thorough hand washing if blood exposure does occur

- Discarding sanitary napkins and tampons into plastic bags

What Else Can Be Done to Prevent the Spread of STDs Among Teens?

In this chapter, we have reviewed numerous ways to protect our teens against the serious epidemic of teen STDs in the U.S.

I urge all parents, educators, and health care professionals to continue to be informed and to seek out new recommendations that may arise in the coming years. For example, CDC guidelines now contain information about pre-exposure prophylaxis (PrEP) against HIV. This is a prevention measure intended for HIV-negative people who are at substantial risk for HIV exposure. I encourage parents to speak to their health care providers to learn more about this intervention.

Over the years, controversy has swirled around the issue of male circumcision—mostly targeting the practice of circumcision in newborn male babies. Estimates vary, but one survey reported that more than 60% of babies are circumcised in the U.S. For years, The American Academy of Pediatrics finds that the health benefits of newborn male circumcision outweigh the risks. However, there are many other aspects to this policy and parents of newborn males will want to have a detailed discussion with their pediatrician.

International studies show that circumcision reduces a male's risk of contracting HIV through heterosexual (male-female) sex by 55 to 76%. Circumcised males are also less likely to transmit HIV to women. And, studies show that circumcision reduces the risk of young men contracting other STDs such as chlamydia and syphilis. The belief is that the warm, moist area under the foreskin of young men who haven't been circumcised provides a breeding ground for infection.

Time will tell if this information will lead to higher percentages of male babies being circumcised. This is just one example of how emerging information may alter medical recommendations at present and in years to come.

Stay tuned!

Chapter 9

Pearls of Wisdom

Follow your instincts. That's where true wisdom manifests itself.

—Oprah Winfrey

From the inception of *Before It's Too Late* to its completion, I have kept one thought in mind—*Follow your instincts*. I knew from my work as an obstetrician/gynecologist and as chairperson of my hospital's program on Teen Pregnancy and STD Prevention, that the topic of teen pregnancy and STD prevention sparks enormous interest in parents.

The previous chapters detailed the issues of teen sexual behavior, teen pregnancy, STDs and their prevention, parenting and communication, and birth control, including abstinence. This chapter highlights, summarizes, and serves as a quick refresher for key points in *Before It's Too Late*.

My Top 20 Pearls of Wisdom for Parents on Teen Pregnancy and STD Prevention

1. Believe That Teen Pregnancy and STDs Are Preventable.

Sometimes problems seem too big to solve. For some, teen pregnancy and STDs fall into that category. I urge you to avoid this type of thinking. Great progress has been made, particularly in the area of teen pregnancy prevention where overall rates have dropped substantially since 1991. It's important to redouble our efforts and to commit to the belief that teen pregnancy and STD infections in teens can be sharply reduced and that this reduction can be sustained.

All Americans should be outraged that U.S. teen pregnancy rates are higher than in many other industrialized countries. ***We can and we must do better!*** Our efforts must be rooted in positive thinking and a heartfelt confidence in our teens and in ourselves.

2. *Be An Empowered Parent.*

Empowered parents are educated and involved in important aspects of their teen's life. They don't sit on the sidelines and watch. By choosing to read *Before It's Too Late*, you have demonstrated your interest in taking proactive steps to guide your teen on this most important subject.

Stay informed about issues that affect your teen, attend school and extracurricular events, and never let your guard down regarding the importance of supervision of your teen, especially during those critical after-school hours. In other words, let your presence be felt.

3. *Recall Your Teen Experiences to Help Put Things in Perspective.*

What stands out in your mind regarding your teen years? Were you the perfect child who never did anything your parents forbade? Did you ever smoke a cigarette or marijuana, drive too fast, or skip a class at school? If so, you weren't alone.

The testing of parental and other limits is normal teen behavior. However, when teens push sexual boundaries, the consequences can be very negative and have a lifelong impact. Teens live in a highly sexualized world and the pressures to have early sex have never been greater.

Incorporate your basic knowledge about teen behavior, relying on your past experiences for perspective, and your understanding of current societal pressures when communicating with and guiding your teen about sex.

4. *Avoid the Peril of Expecting Perfection.*

One of the most common sentiments expressed by parents is that they don't know how to talk to their kids about sex and they don't know what to say. Becoming a more informed parent will certainly help to boost your confidence. However, part of the difficulty is that too many parents are afraid of saying the wrong thing or making a comment their teen will find confusing.

Parents don't have to be perfect to effectively guide their teens about sex. Your ability to express your care and concern for your teen will speak volumes. If you say something you later regret or feel was incorrect, be willing to admit it and start over. Your teen will not only appreciate your honesty, but by example you will have given your child the freedom to admit mistakes as well.

5. *Praise Before Pointing Fingers.*

How often are teens depicted for the problems they create and not for the many incredible joys they bring to their friends, families, and communities? Most national news is negative in nature (tragic accidents, colossal storms, troubling national debt, death due to war, etc.). Focusing on the positive does not seem to be consistent with our human nature.

You will need to reverse this tendency in order to motivate your teens and guide them about sex. By emphasizing their positive traits, you can enhance your teens' self-esteem and connect with them in more meaningful ways, which can help to reduce risky sexual behavior.

If your teen is a great listener or has a keen sense of humor, let him/her know that you recognize and appreciate this. Give praise for a good grade on an exam or a solid sports performance. And when you need to give constructive criticism, surround it with positive language and they'll be much more likely to absorb what you have to say. For example—"I think it's great that you have so many friends and that you have such an easygoing and fun personality. However, when you're at school, it's important that you pay attention to your teacher and not talk to your friends until class is over."

6. *Keep Talking.*

In the past, many parents and teens took part in "The Talk"—that profound discussion about "the birds and bees" when kids were taught how babies were made and what was proper when it came to sex.

We now know that preteens and teens generally hate "The Talk" and that it did little good anyhow. Not only were all parties uncomfortable with "The Talk," but there was an assumption that one, heart-to-heart conversation was all it took to cover what your kids needed to know about sex.

Communication with your children about sex should be an ongoing conversation. Even very enlightened parents who have open relationships with their kids can have a false sense of security. There are ample examples of parents who thought their teen was using birth control—only to learn that the teen ran out and didn't refill the prescription, or who assumed that because their teen pointedly told them he or she was not having sex that this meant oral sex as well.

Protecting our kids from the negative consequences of sex means never letting down our guard!

7. *Reduce the Risk with Information.*

In my experience as a physician and as chairperson of a Teen Pregnancy and STD Prevention Program, I have been frequently surprised at the lack of knowledge about sexual health among teens. Often, teens say they've heard about an STD like HPV or chlamydia, but they have no idea about what an infection with one of these could mean for them. Rarely do teens really comprehend, before they get pregnant, the life-changing impact teen pregnancy brings or the health risks for them and their children.

I urge parents to review the information presented in this book with their children and to support pregnancy and STD prevention programs.

8. *Remember That Respect and Responsibility Rule.*

Encouraging teens to respect themselves and to take responsibility for their actions is a critical component of effective parenting. Teens with a high degree of respect and care for themselves are less likely to engage in risky sexual behavior. And teens who think highly of themselves are less concerned about what others think, and more immune to peer pressure about sex and other issues.

Responsibility and obedience in a teen are not necessarily the same thing. The 100% obedient child probably doesn't exist. On the other hand, teens can be guided to make being responsible a standard in their lives (e.g., teens who do not heed parents' advice about delaying sex, but who accept responsibility for using birth control, ideally dual contraception that includes condoms).

9. *Help Your Teen Know What Love Is and What Love Isn't.*

Teens may mistake the romantic feelings associated with a crush for "true love," and this may cause them to feel that sex is OK. Some will feel not only heartache, but regret, for having acted on what they falsely perceived as feelings of "love" when in fact they were infatuated.

Parents are in a unique position to help their children learn what real love entails; not just romance, but kindness, commitment, and often placing the other person's needs first, to name a few.

Parents also want to stress to their teens that love should never include abusive behavior—emotional, physical, or sexual.

10. *Keep Learning and Be Aware of New Trends in Teen Behavior.*

Who had ever heard of "rainbow parties"—where teen girls wearing different colored lipsticks give boys oral sex at parties—when today's parents were teens? Now we have sexting—where nude photos or sexually explicit messages are communicated by cell phones. What will be the next trend to cause parental angst?

Technology has ushered in a whole new arena for teens to receive and give what are often inappropriate messages and images. The viewing of sexually explicit or pornographic material is now much more accessible.

Parenting now means not just knowing and monitoring teens' TV viewing, but personal computers, cell phones, Blackberries, etc. Parents will want to place parental controls on media content that they find objectionable.

11. *Promote Activities and Behaviors Shown to Help Teens Delay Sex.*

Parents must work more diligently than ever to combat the messages our teens receive, in large doses, in our highly sexualized society. Not only does "sex sell," but sex in the media is frequently portrayed without the use of birth control, and unintended pregnancy and STDs are not often part of the story line. All the while, sex scandals provide ongoing fodder for cable news.

There are many steps that parents can take to reduce the chances their teens will engage in early and/or risky sex. These include encouraging their participation in extracurricular activities, sports, volunteer services, and religious activities, as well as setting high goals for themselves.

In addition, parents can discourage early dating, boyfriends/girlfriends who are much older (e.g., three years), and hanging out with older friends. And knowing your kids' friends and their parents is important, too.

12. *Support Birth Control Information as a Right for Every Teen.*

Knowledge is not harmful, but ignorance most definitely can be. Some teens get pregnant because they believe myths like, "You won't get pregnant the first time you have sex." Or, they don't use condoms correctly.

The education of teens about birth control, including abstinence or delaying sex, should be a basic human right. And providing such information has not been shown to increase the likelihood that teens will engage in sex.

Parents, along with educators and health care providers, must work diligently to guarantee that every U.S. teen understands the basics of birth control—along with reading, writing, and arithmetic.

13. Help Teens Avoid Underage Drinking and Illegal Drug Use.

Most parents are familiar with stories detailing the tragic outcomes resulting from teens involved in underage drinking or drug use—the prom night car crash leaving lifeless, mangled bodies and shattered families; cocaine or methamphetamine use that spirals into addiction and ultimately suicide; poor school performance or dropping out of school altogether.

Studies also show that drinking or drug use significantly increases the risk that teens will participate in early and unprotected sex or become a victim of adolescent dating violence or date rape.

The message against underage drinking and illegal drug use among teens must be loud and pervasive. It's a message our teens cannot afford to ignore!

14. Emphasize Your Values and Morals.

Parents are the primary sex educators of their children. Teens may receive more formal instruction at school or in a health care provider's office, but parents must shoulder the huge job of communicating their values regarding sex. When parents fail to do this, kids receive their values by default from their peers or the media.

In order to do this, parents must first clarify their values and morals pertaining to teens and sex. Sometimes, parents may have mixed feelings or might regret some of their own decisions about sex in the past. This should not deter them from determining where they stand now and being able to communicate what they feel is appropriate to their teens. Don't relegate this all-too-important aspect of sex education to anyone else!

15. *Be Approachable and Remain Ever-Vigilant.*

Being effective in guiding your teens about sexual behavior isn't just about you talking and your teen listening. You want your teen to come to you with questions and concerns.

The best way to insure that your teen will be comfortable in coming to you is to be an approachable parent. There may be many ways of describing an approachable parent, but here's what tops my list—good listener, nonjudgmental, confidential, warm, calm, lighthearted, and open-minded.

16. *Listen and Speak with Love.*

In our fast-paced, technologically advanced, and goal-oriented society, it can be easy to overlook the most important guiding force that we, as parents own—our love for our children. Loving our teens and expressing that love are not synonymous.

It's important to let our teens know, often, that they are special and precious to us and that our love for them is unconditional. When our teens are certain of this love, they are more likely to listen to and heed our advice. For even when they roll their eyes at our comments or tell us that they "hate us," the love bond that we have forged will always be there, like an anchor that keeps them steady.

17. *Never Underestimate Parental Influence.*

Survey after survey confirms this basic tenet—teens really do care about what their parents think and say. Think about it—how often are children swayed by their parents' choices on important issues like politics, education, and religion?

Why should parental sway be any different in determining teen sex behavior? It isn't. When it comes to sex, parents do influence, but do not control, the decisions that teens make.

Parents are encouraged to take advantage of the many teachable moments that occur in life to get their message about sex across to their kids. These moments can arise while watching a TV show or movie, listening to the radio, responding to another teen's predicament resulting from an unwise decision about sex, and in many other situations.

18. Support Teens in Talking with Other Responsible Adults.

This pearl of wisdom may seem at odds with the others on this list, but it is a very important one to keep in mind. The majority of parents and teens find talking about sex awkward and uncomfortable. This is normal. However, it's up to parents to make the effort and to be approachable, which can open the door to healthy and more comfortable communication about sex.

However, in some cases and for a host of different reasons, teens will want to direct their questions and concerns to another responsible adult—a relative or family friend. Parents should support such efforts by their teens. The key is to avoid taking this personally and to remember that ensuring that your teen receives accurate sex information is what counts.

19. Partner with Health Care Providers and Educators.

The American College of Obstetricians and Gynecologists recommends that teen girls should be seen by a health care provider specializing in reproductive health between the ages of 13 and 15. This visit allows your teen to become acquainted with and comfortable with her provider. Safe general health practices can be enforced and sexual health issues addressed. In many cases, teens will not need an exam, STD testing, or birth control at this first visit. However, an important relationship will be established to assist in educating your teen about sexual health.

Teen boys should also be seen, usually by their pediatrician or family care provider, to address sexual health.

The school system also serves as an important source of guidance for our teens regarding sex education. As discussed in Chapter 6, America is moving toward a more Comprehensive Sex Education approach for teens. Together with parents and health care providers, our education system provides an essential ingredient— helping to insure that all children receive basic and accurate sex information.

20. *Take Advantage of Outside and Community Resources.*

There are numerous organizations, hotlines, and websites that provide ongoing parenting information about teens and sex. Key resources are listed in Chapter 10, and I welcome you to visit my website, **www.droverton.org.** Parents are encouraged to take advantage of the resources available and to consider creative ways to help teens make healthier and smarter decisions about sex. Examples include joining together with other interested parents to voice concerns about an issue like adolescent dating violence in your community or starting a petition to address an issue like objectionable sex content on a prime time television show.

It will take all of us—parents, educators, health care professionals, policymakers, clergy and concerned citizens everywhere, caring about the health and well-being of our children and putting our words into action to drastically and permanently decrease teen pregnancy rates, eradicate the STD epidemic among U.S. teens, and safeguard the futures of our most precious resource—our children. ***Together, we can and we must make a difference—before it's too late!***

Chapter 10

You Are Not Alone: Support Made Simple

Reducing teen pregnancy and the incidence of STDs among teens in the U.S. must remain a top priority for parents, educators, and health care professionals. The combined efforts of each of these groups are needed to give our children the best possible opportunity to reach their full potential, unhindered by the consequences of early and/or risky sexual behavior.

In this chapter, you will find key resources for the topics addressed in this book. While other resources are available, those listed represent organizations, programs, and websites with the most comprehensive information. These references will serve as valuable stepping stones as you take the information presented in *Before It's Too Late* further and continue on the path—protecting and guiding your children.

Comprehensive Information on Teen Pregnancy and Prevention

1. **National Campaign to Prevent Teen and Unplanned Pregnancy**

   1776 Massachusetts Ave. NW, Ste. 200
   Washington, DC 20036
   202-478-8500 (P)
   202-478-8588 (F)
   www.teenpregnancy.org
   www.stayteen.org (emphasis on teen attitudes/values)

   The National Campaign to Prevent Teen and Unplanned Pregnancy was founded in 1996 as the National

Campaign to Prevent Teen Pregnancy. It serves as the most far-reaching and influential source of information on teen pregnancy prevention. Its goal of decreasing teen pregnancy in the U.S. by one-third during its first 10 years of operation has been largely successful.

- Offers a wealth of information for parents and teens

- Provides accurate information on all aspects of teen pregnancy with an emphasis on national surveys and research findings

- Provides a balanced approach to the issue of teen pregnancy prevention and stresses responsible teen values and behavior

- Offers specific recommendations to teens and parents, including many tips for building stronger communication between teens and parents

- Gives current, frequently updated information on national/state trends regarding teen sex attitudes and behavior, as well as teen pregnancy

- Includes perspectives from policymakers, educators, entertainment personnel, faith-based communities, and more

2. Healthy Teen Network

1501 Saint Paul St., Ste. 124
Baltimore, MD 21201
410-685-0410 (P)
410-685-0481 (F)
www.healthyteennetwork.org

Healthy Teen Network, founded in 1979 as the National Association on Adolescent Pregnancy, Parenting and Prevention, serves to promote both teen pregnancy prevention and successful teen parenting and families.

- Uses a comprehensive approach

- Provides education opportunities for reproductive health care professionals through networking, information sharing, and training

- Promotes science-based programs and policy

Comprehensive Information—Teen Sexual Behavior, Teen Pregnancy, and STDs

1. **Advocates for Youth**

   200 M St. NW, Ste. 750
   Washington, DC 20036
   202-419-3420 (P)
   202-419-1448 (F)
   www.AdvocatesforYouth

   Advocates for Youth is an organization that works in the U.S. as well as in developing countries to "champion efforts to help young people make informed and responsible decisions about their reproductive and sexual health."

   - Stresses three core values: Rights, Respect, and Responsibility

   - Promotes teen pregnancy prevention

   - Offers strategies related to STD prevention: Current initiatives include a focus on Youth of Color as well as Gay, Lesbian, and Bisexual Youth

   - Provides specific advice for teens as well as parents

- Features in their parent section include: Are You an Askable Parent? What to Do When They Just Won't Talk

2. **Campaign for Our Children**

   One North Charles St., 11ᵗʰ Fl.
   Baltimore, MD 21201
   410-576-9015 (P)
   410-756-7075 (F)
   www.cfoc.org

   Campaign for Our Children was founded in 1987 to combat the high rate of teen pregnancy. A central part of Campaign for Our Children's mission is to "develop research-based prevention messages and educational campaigns which encourage healthy, responsible decisions among adolescents."

   - Offers a "Teen Guide" which covers subjects from abstinence to date rape drugs

   - Provides a "Parent Resource Center" with tips on Talking with Kids About Sex and more

   - Supports educators with resource information

Information on Sexually Transmitted Diseases

1. **Centers for Disease Control and Prevention**

   1600 Clifton Road
   Atlanta, GA 30333
   888-232-6348
   www.cdc.gov

The Centers for Disease Control and Prevention (CDC) is the nation's premier source of medically accurate information about STDs. It is a governmental agency and a division of the Department of Health and Human Services.

- Advances national health and disease prevention

- Provides the latest information on STDs with up-to-date statistics and research findings

- Presents easy-to-understand information for individuals, health professionals, and educators

- Provides specific information about STD testing, including locations of STD clinic sites at **www.hivtest.org**

2. **American Social Health Association**

P.O. Box 13827
Research Triangle Park, NC 27709
919-361-8400 (P)
919-361-8425 (F)
www.asha

The American Social Health Association is a nonprofit organization, founded in 1914, which promotes awareness of STIs (sexually transmitted infections/diseases).

- Provides educational materials on STIs and their prevention

- Offers STI hotlines, resources for support, and referrals

STD Hotlines

1. **Centers for Disease Control**
    800-232-3228

2. **National STD Hotline**
    800-227-8922 (English/Spanish)

3. **National AIDS Hotline**
    800-344-7432 (English/Spanish/TTY)
    800-243-7889 (English/Spanish/TTY)

4. **National HPV/Cervical Cancer Prevention Hotline**
    919-361-4848

5. **Herpes Resource Center**
    919-361-2120

STD Brochures

1. **STD Facts—Sexually Transmitted Diseases, #153**
2. **PID-Pelvic Inflammatory Disease, #187**
3. **HIV Facts, #H196**
4. **STD Testing—Stay STD Free, #043**

    P.O. Box 1830
    Santa Cruz, CA 95061-1830
    800-321-4407
    www.etr.org

5. **Condoms and Sexually Transmitted Disease Brochure**

www.fda.gov/ForConsumers/byAudience/
ForPatientAdvocates/HIVandAIDSActivities/uc m126372.
htm

Information on Abstinence

1. **Parents For Truth**

   1701 Pennsylvania Ave. NW, Ste. 300
   Washington, DC 20006
   202-248-5420 (P)
   202-580-6559 (F)
   www.parentsfortruth.org

   A recently formed organization by The National
   Abstinence Education Association, Parents For Truth
   supports abstinence education.

   • Provides parents and teens with resources to promote
     sexual abstinence until marriage

   • Seeks to motivate and empower teens to make good
     health decisions and to avoid risky behaviors

   • Advances the philosophy of abstinence education
     for young people in broader terms to include the
     promotion of healthy relationships and the setting of
     goals, in addition to providing some information about
     STDs and birth control

2. **True Love Waits**

   One LifeWay Plaza
   Nashville, TN 37234
   615-251-2000
   www.lifeway.com

Founded by Dr. Richard Ross and Jimmy Hester, this philosophy is Christian-based and promotes sexual abstinence for young people until marriage.

- Encourages youth to make a commitment (pledge) to remain abstinent until marriage

- Uses Biblical verses to support its principles

- Provides tips for parenting teens and marriage advice

Abstinence Brochures

1. **Talking with Your Teen About Abstinence, #H135**
2. **101 Ways to Make Love Without Doing It, #063**

   P.O. Box 1830
   Santa Cruz, CA 95061-1830
   800-321-4407
   www.etr.org

Information on Birth Control

1. **Planned Parenthood**

   434 West 33rd St.
   New York, NY 10001
   212-245-7800 or 800-230-7526 (P)
   212-245-1845 (F)
   www.plannedparenthood.org
   (click "The Facts on Birth Control")

   Founded more than 90 years ago, Planned Parenthood provides comprehensive reproductive health care services, sex education, and information to a worldwide audience.

- Operates local, community-based health centers

- Serves as a passionate advocate at the local, national, and international level for comprehensive sexual health care for young people

- Provides specific tools for parents and educators

- Offers a special section, Teen Talk

2. Center for Young Women's Health

333 Longwood Ave., 5th Fl.
Boston, MA 02115
617-355-2994 (P)
617-730-0186 (F)
www.youngwomenshealth.org
(click "Sexuality & Health")

This clinic offers an interactive website designed for teens. It provides information on birth control and a host of reproductive health issues for teens and parents.

- Discusses the different options for birth control including the pros/cons of each method

- Includes topics ranging from abstinence to nutrition and fitness

3. Office of Population Affairs

www.hhs.gov/opa/
240-453-2888

This governmental office provides information about the Title X Family Planning Program which provides birth control assistance for low-income teens and families.

Contraception—Miscellaneous Information

1. **Emergency Contraception (It's Not Too Late)**
   www.path.org/publications/details.php?i=1246

2. **Know Your CONDOM DOs & DON'Ts**
   http://www.cdc.gov/teenpregnancy/pdf/teen-condom-fact-sheet-2015.pdf

Information on Teen Sexual Assault/ Adolescent Dating Violence

1. **Futures Without Violence**

   100 Montgomery Street,
   The Presidio
   San Francisco, CA 94129
   415-678-5500 (P)
   415-529-2930 (F)
   www.futureswithoutviolence.org

   Formerly known as the Family Violence Prevention Fund, Futures Without Violence works to prevent violence within the home and communities.

   • Specific Teen Program targets include dating violence and reproductive coercion

   • Promotes awareness of physical, verbal, and sexual abuse

   • Advocates for public policy measures that protect teens from all aspects of intimate partner violence

Top Websites/Helplines

1. www.loveisrespect.org

- Provides information about healthy dating relationships

- Defines abusive dating relationships and the warning signs

- Works to stop the spread of digital abuse

- Offers support and education for parents

- Provides 24-hour helpline staffed by trained peer advocates

- Helpline Phone: 866-331-9474

Brochures

- Dating: What's Normal, What's Not, #R839

- Date Rape: Teens Talk with Teens, #154

- Sexual Violence, #H212

P.O. Box 1830
Santa Cruz, CA 95061-1830
800-321-4407
www.etr.org

Professional Medical Organizations

1. **American College of Obstetricians and Gynecologists**

   PO Box 96920
   Washington, DC 20090-6920
   202-638-5577
   www.acog.org

   The American College of Obstetricians and Gynecologists (ACOG) provides the quality standards and guidelines for the nation's obstetricians and gynecologists. It is devoted to ensuring that women of all ages receive the best possible health care.

   • Offers an Adolescent Pregnancy Prevention Network which coordinates efforts among health care professionals to reduce teen pregnancy

   • Educates its members and the public regarding the challenging issues involved in women's health care

   • Serves as a strong voice advocating for women's health care

   • Provides referrals for obstetricians and gynecologists

2. **Society of Adolescent Medicine**

   111 Deer Lake Road, Ste. 100
   Deerfield, IL 60015
   847-753-5226 (P)
   847-480-9282 (F)
   www.adolescenthealth.org

   This organization consists of health professionals from multiple specialties. It is "committed to advancing the health and well-being of adolescents."

- Addresses a broad range of issues from body image and sexuality to substance abuse and family or school concerns

- Promotes awareness of adolescent health matters among professionals and the lay public

- Provides teen and family resources

- Offers referral services

2. **American Academy of Pediatrics**

   141 Northwest Point Blvd.
   Elk Grove Village, IL 60007
   847-434-4000 (P)
   847-434-8000 (F)
   www.aap.org

   The American Academy of Pediatrics is the leading professional organization for pediatricians, and is dedicated to providing the best possible health care and well-being for patients from infancy to young adulthood.

   - Provides a special section for parents and teens on adolescent sexual health (click "healthychildren. org")

   - Develops policies and guidelines for health care professionals who care for children and adolescents

   - Provides referrals for pediatricians

Community Resources for Children and Adolescents

1. **YMCA (Young Men's Christian Association)**

   YMCA of the USA
   101 North Wacker Drive

Chicago, IL 60606
800-872-9622
www.ymca.net

As one of the nation's largest nonprofit community service organizations, the YMCA serves millions of children and adults from all faiths and backgrounds. At its core is its mission to "partner with families to build strong kids and strong communities."

- Helps children and youth develop positive values

- Offers a wealth of activities for youth—including sports, camping, and educational programs

- Provides numerous resources for families, including parenting guides

2. **Big Brothers Big Sisters of America**

230 North 13th St.
Philadelphia, PA 19107
215-567-7000 (P)
215-567-0394 (F)
www.bbbs.org

This is the nation's oldest mentoring organization. The relationships it provides create a lifelong, positive impact for the children it serves.

- Provides mentoring for children and adolescents from 6 to 18

- Coordinates the establishment of one-to-one mentoring with caring adults

- Has been shown to improve school performance and decrease drug and alcohol use among its participants

3. **4-H Club**

www.4-h.org

(click "Join 4-H" to locate club near you)

This national organization for youth emphasizes life skills, knowledge, and character.

- Promotes the fourfold development of youth: head, heart, hands, and health

- Its core mission mandates are: healthy living, citizenship, and science, engineering, and technology

- Relies heavily on caring adult volunteers

4. **Girls Incorporated**

120 Wall Street
New York, NY 10005
212-509-2000 (P)
212-509-8708
www.girlsinc.org

This is one of the leading organizations dedicated to supporting girls and positive development. It reached national status in 1945. Its credo inspires all girls to be "strong, smart, and bold".

- Encourages girls to realize their full potential

- Inspires girls to value and assert their rights

- Provides research-based programs that allow girls to master physical, intellectual and emotional, challenges.

5. **Boys & Girls Clubs of America**

1275 Peachtree Street, NE
Atlanta, GA 30309-3506
Phone: 404-487-5700
www.bgca.org

This organization was begun in 1860 by three women who wanted to provide a positive alternative to boys who roamed the streets. It boasts thousands of clubs throughout the country and serves a diverse population.

- Provides a safe environment for boys and girls to learn and grow

- Offers support from caring, adult professionals

- Strengthens character and encourages hope and opportunity

*Parents are also encouraged to search your local community for youth and recreational services.

Other Resources

1. **School-Based Teen Pregnancy and STD Prevention Programs**

   The vast majority of Teen Pregnancy and STD Prevention Programs are school-based. They are effectively able to reach kids because their services are provided on the school campus. Many different programs exist throughout the country. A detailed description of the most effective programs, based on scientific study, is beyond the scope of this book.

   Parents are encouraged to visit the website for The National Campaign to Prevent Teen and Unplanned Pregnancy at **www.teenpregnancy.org** and are referred to "What Works: Curriculum-Based Programs That Prevent Teen Pregnancy."

   Parents may inquire about more specific information on school-based Teen Pregnancy and STD Prevention

Programs in their community by contacting their state Department of Public Health or Board of Education.

3. **Community-Based Teen Pregnancy and STD Prevention Programs**

   Community-based programs that focus exclusively on Teen Pregnancy and/or STD Prevention are few in number. One such program will be highlighted in this section.

   Carrera Adolescent Pregnancy Prevention Program
   www.stopteenpregnancy.com

   Founded in 1984 by Dr. Carrera and The Children's Aid Society, The Carrera Adolescent Pregnancy Prevention Program offers a "holistic and long-term" approach to teen pregnancy prevention. This holistic approach recognizes that many factors such as school success, access to medical care, and positive role models are important in teen pregnancy prevention.

   - Offers parent participation

   - Includes support in education, employment, medical/dental assistance, family life, and sex education

References

Introduction

Guttmacher Institute. Fact Sheet. American Teens' Sexual and Reproductive Health. May 2014. www.guttmacher.org/pubs/FB-ATSRH.html.

Centers for Disease Control and Prevention Fact Sheet: Information for Teens and Young Adults: Staying Healthy and Preventing STDs, Updated 2015 www.cdc.gov/std/life-stages-populations/STDFact-Teens.htm.

Forhan, S. E., et al. 2009. Prevalence of sexually transmitted infections among female adolescents aged 14-19 in the United States. *Pediatrics* 124(6): 1505-1512.

Chapter 1

Behar, J. 2010. Interview with teens from MTV's "16 and Pregnant." February 10, 2010.

Beckett, M., et al. 2010. Timing of parent and child communication about sexuality relative to children's sexual behaviors. *Pediatrics* 125:34-42.

Martinez, P. 2010. My family life: Chris Meloni. *Family Circle*, February 10, 2010: 204.

Wilson, E., et al. 2010. Parents' perspectives on talking to preteenage children about sex. *Perspectives on Sexual and Reproductive Health* 42:56-63.

Chapter 2

Ackard, D. A., et al. 2007. Long-term impact of adolescent dating violence on the behavioral and psychological health of male and female youth. *Journal of Pediatrics* 151(5):476–81.

Albert, B., et al. 2005. Freeze frame: a snapshot of America's teens. The National Campaign to Prevent Teen and Unplanned Pregnancy. www.thenationalcampaign.org/resources/pdf/pubs/FreezeFrame.pdf.

Albert, B. 2012. With One Voice. America's Adults And Teens Sound Off About Teen Pregnancy. http://thenationalcampaign.org/resource/one-voice-2012.

Albert, B., S. Brown, and C. Flanigan, eds. 2003. 14 and younger: the sexual behavior of young adolescents. (Summary). Washington, DC: National Campaign to Prevent Teen Pregnancy.

Allan Guttmacher Institute. 2006. Teenagers' sexual and reproductive health: developed countries. www.guttmacher.org.

American College of Obstetricians and Gynecologists. 2013. Addressing Health Risks of Noncoital Sexual Activity. ACOG Committee Opinion No. 582.

Bechtel, L. K., and C. P. Holstege. 2007. Criminal poisoning: drug facilitated sexual assault. *Emergency Clinics of North America* 25(2):499–525.

Centers for Disease Control and Prevention. Understanding Teen Dating Violence. Fact Sheet 2014. www.cdc.gov/violenceprevention/pdf/teen-dating-violence-2014-a.pdf

Chandra, A., et al. 2008. Does watching sex on television predict teen pregnancy? Findings from a national longitudinal survey on youth. *Pediatrics* 122(5): 1047–54.

Coffey, L. 2008. Survey: unprotected sex common among teens. http://today.msnbc.com/id/27706917/.

Friedan, T., Jaffe, H., Cono, J., et al. Youth Risk Behavior Surveillance—United States 2013. Centers for Disease Control and Prevention www.cdc.gov/mmwr/PDF/ss/ss6304.pdf

Eaton, K., et al. 2008. Trends in the prevalence of sexual behaviors. National YRBS: 1991–2007. Centers for Disease Control and Prevention. www.cdc.gov/HealthyYouth/yrbs/pdf/yrbs07_us_sexual_behaviors_trend.pdf.

Futures Without Violence. The Facts on Tween and Teens and Dating Violence, Emerging Issues Facing Tweens and Teens (2013) www.futureswithoutviolence.org.

Gilda, S., et al. 2015. Adolescent Pregnancy, Birth, and Abortion Rates Across Countries: Levels and Recent Trends. *Journal of Adolescent Health* 56(2): 223-230.

Gunter, J. 2007. Intimate partner violence. *Obstetrics & Gynecology Clinics* 34(3):367–88.

Kaiser Permanente West Los Angeles Teen Pregnancy Prevention Seminars, 1998–2007.

Kirby D. 2007. Emerging answers 2007: research findings on programs to reduce teen pregnancy and STDs. National Campaign to Prevent Teen and Unplanned Pregnancy. www.teenpregnancy.org.

———. 2007. Sexual risk and protective factors. National Campaign to Prevent Teen and Unplanned Pregnancy. www.thenationalcampaign.org/ea2007/protective_factors_SUM.pdf.

Lemay, C. A., et al. 2007. Adolescent mother's attitudes toward contraception before and after pregnancy. *J. Ped. Adol. Gyn.* 20(4):233–40.

Manlove, J., et al. 2003. A good time: after-school programs to reduce teen pregnancy. National Campaign to Prevent Teen Pregnancy. www.thenationalcampaign.org/resources/pdf/pubs/AGoodTime.pdf.

Mojola, S. and Everette, B. 2012. STD and HIV risk factors among U.S. young adults: variations by race, ethnicity, and sexual orientation. *Perspectives on Sexual and Reproductive Health* 44 (22): 125-133.

National Campaign to Prevent Teen and Unplanned Pregnancy. 2009. Sex and technology. www.thenationalcampaign.org/sextech.

———. 2005. Science says: teens' attitudes toward sex, 2002. http://thenationalcampaign.org/resource/science-says-14.

———. 2007. Science says: the sexual behavior of young adolescents. thenationalcampaign.org/resource/science-says-33.

———. 2003. Science says: where and when teens first have sex. http://thenationalcampaign.org/resource/science-says-1.

———. 2003. 14 and younger: new report examines sexual behavior of young adolescents. www.thenationalcampaign.org/resources/reports.aspx.

———. 2005. The cautious generation: teens having less sex and using contraception more. www.thenationalcampaign.org/about-us/PDF/Spring2005update.pdf.

Parker-Pope, T. 2009. The myth of rampant teenage promiscuity. *The New York Times*. January 27, 2009, D6.

Roberts, S. T. 2006. Why are young college women not using condoms? Their perceived risk, drug use and developmental vulnerability may provide important clues to sexual risk. *Archives Psychiatric Nursing* 20(1):32–40.

Sanders, S. A. and J. M. Reinisch. 1999. What is sex? (Is it really sex?). *JAMA* 281(3):275–72.

Strasburger, V. C., et al. 2010. Health effects of media on children and adolescents. *Pediatrics* 125;756–767. www.pediatrics.org/cgi/content/full/125/4/756.

Strasburger, V. C. 2006. Risky business: what primary care practitioners need to know about the influence of the media on adolescents. *Primary Care: Clinics in Office Practice* 33(2):317–48.

Whitehead, B.D., et al. 2001. Keeping the faith: the role of religion and faith communities in preventing teen pregnancy. www.thenationalcampaign.org/resources/pdf/pubs/KeepingFaith_FINAL.pdf.

Wolitzky-Taylor, K. B., et al. 2008. Prevalence and correlates of dating violence in a national sample of adolescents. *J. Am. Acad. of Child and Adol. Psych.* 47(7):755–62.

Chapter 3

Adolescent childbearing and educational and economic attainment. 2008. www.advocatesforyouth.org/news/index.php?option=com_content&task=view&id=412&Itemid=336.

Allan Guttmacher Institute. 2010. Facts on American teens' sexual and reproductive health. www.guttmacher.org/pubs/fb_ATSRH.html.

———. 2001. Teenagers' sexual and reproductive health in developed countries. www.guttmacher.org.

Allen, C. A. 2003. Peer pressure and teen sex. *Psychology Today.* www.psychologytoday.com/articles/pto-20030522-000002.html.

Ayoola, A., et al. 2006. Epidemiology and prevention of unintended pregnancy in adolescents. *Primary Care: Clinics in Office Practice* 33(2):391–403.

Boschert, S. 2008. Pregnant teen higher risk factors quantified. *Ob-Gyn News* 43(12):13.

———. 2008. Preterm birth risk in depressed teens. *Ob-Gyn News* 43(13):1–6.

Britney Spears' mother: 'It's been a whirlwind.' 2008. today.msnbc.msn.com/id/26735043.

Brown, S. 2003. Letter to the White House Task Force on Disadvantaged Youth. www.thenationalcampaign.org/policymakers/PDF/whyouth.pdf.

Casazza, K., et al. 2008. Associations among insulin, estrogen, and fat mass gain over the pubertal transition in African-American and European-American girls. *J. Clin. Endocrin. and Metab.* 93(7):2610–15. jcem.endojournals.org/cgi/content/abstract/jc.2007-2776v1.

Eugster, E., and M. Palmert. 2006. Precocious puberty. *J. Clin. Endocrin. and Metab.* 91 (9): 151–16A. jcem.endojournals.org/cgi/content/full/91/9/0.

Futures Without Violence. www.futureswithoutviolence.org

Hamilton, B. E., et al. 2014. Births: preliminary data for 2013. National vital statistics reports. National Center for Health Statistics. www.cdc.gov/nchs/data/nvsr/nvsr63/nvsr63_02.pdf

Kane, A. 2008. The power of prevention. Spotlight On Poverty. www.spotlightonpoverty.org/ExclusiveCommentary.aspx?id=472711fe-6c23-4674-af23-98e0ee87454b.

Kingsbury, K. 2008. Postcard: Gloucester. How one school is grappling with the Juno effect. *Time.* www.time.com/time/world/article/0,8599,1815845,00.html?cnn=yes.

Kirby, D., and G. Lepore. 2007. Sexual risk and protective factors. National Campaign to Prevent Teen Pregnancy. www.thenationalcampaign.org/EA2007/protective_factors_SUM.pdf.

Melanie Knight tells us how she became a successful college graduate. *College Mom Magazine.* 2008; II(2).

Most, D. 2005. *Always in our hearts: The story of Amy Grossberg, Brian Peterson.* New York: St. Martin's Press.

National Campaign to Prevent Teen and Unplanned Pregnancy. 2013. Teen Childbearing in Rural America. http://thenationalcampaign. org/sites/default/files/resource-primary-download/ss47_ teenchildbearinginruralamerica.pdf.

———. 2012. Why it matters. Teen Childbearing, Education, and Economic Wellbeing. http://thenationalcampaign.org/resource/ why-it-matters-teen-childbearing-education-and-economic-wellbeing.

———. Why it matters: Teen Pregnancy http://thenationalcampaign. org/why-it-matters/teen-pregnancy.

———. 2007. Why it matters: Teen pregnancy and violence (archived resources). http://thenationalcampaign.org/resource/why-it-matters-teen-pregnancy-and-violence.

———. 2007. Why it matters: Teen Pregnancy and overall child well-being. http://thenationalcampaign.org/resource/why-it-matters-teen-pregnancy-and-overall-child-wellbeing.

———. Why it matters: Teen pregnancy, out-of-wedlock births, healthy relationships, and marriage. www.thenationalcampaign. org/why-it-matters/pdf/marriage.pdf.

Seelye, K. Q. 2008. Palin's teen daughter is pregnant; new G.O.P. tumult. *New York Times*, September 1, 2008.

Wolke, A. 2008. Teen pregnancy prevention: What role are states playing? *National Conference of State Legislatures* 29(510):1–3.

Chapter 4

American College of Obstetricians and Gynecologists. 2016. Cervical Cancer Screening and Prevention. ACOG Practice Bulletin: 157

Avert.org. 2010. Personal stories of young people living with HIV. www.avert.org/hiv-stories.htm.

Batalden, K., et al. 2007. Genital herpes and the teen female. *J. Ped. Adol. Gyn.* 20(6):1–3.

Centers for Disease Control and Prevention. Chlamydia fact sheet. www.cdc.gov/std/chlamydia/STDFact-Chlamydia.htm.

———. Genital herpes fact sheet. www.cdc.gov/std/Herpes/STDFact-Herpes.htm.

———. Genital HPV infection fact sheet. www.cdc.gov/std/HPV/STDFact-HPV.htm.

———. Gonorrhea fact sheet. www.cdc.gov/std/Gonorrhea/STDFact-gonorrhea.htm.

———. Hepatitis B-frequently asked questions. www.cdc.gov/hepatitis/HBV.

———. HIV Among Youth. (updated 2015) http://www.cdc.gov/hiv/group/age/youth/index/html.

———. HIV Surveillance-Adolescents and Young Adults. www.cdc.gov/hiv/pdf/statistics_surveillance_adolescents.pdf.

———. Oral sex and HIV risk. www.cdc.gov/hiv/resources/factsheets/oralsex.htm.

———. Reported AIDS cases among adolescents 13–19 years of age, by sex, 1985-2007. www.cdc.gov/hiv/topics/surveillance/resources/slides/adolescents.

———. 2013. CDC Fact Sheet. Incidence, Prevalence, and Cost of Sexually Transmitted Infections in the United States. www.cdc.gov/std/stats/sti-estimates-fact-sheet-Feb-2013.pdf

———. 2015. Sexually Transmitted Disease Treatment Guidelines. MMWR. www.cdc/std/tg2015/ts-2015-print.pdf.

———. 2008. Sexually transmitted diseases in the United States, 2008. www.cdc.gov/std/stats08/trends.htm.

———. 2007. Sexually transmitted disease surveillance, 2007. www.cdc.gov/std/stats07/adol.htm.

———. STD surveillance 2007. www.cdc.gov/std/stats07/gonorrhea.htm#17.

———. STD surveillance 2007 adolescents and young adults. www.cdc.gov/std/stats07/adol.htm.

———. Tracking the hidden epidemics-trends in STDs in the United States-2000. www.cdc.gov/std/trends2000/trends2000.

————. Improvements in sexual and reproductive health of teens and young adults slowing. www.cdc.gov/media/pressrel/2009/r090716a.htm.

Chiaradonna, C. 2008. The chlamydia cascade: enhanced STD prevention strategies for adolescents. *J. Ped. Adol. Gyn.* 21(5):336. www.mdconsult.com/das/article/body/179871611-18/jorg=journal&source=MI&sp=21007111&sid=943615886/N/661877/1.html?issn-1083-3188.

Cohen, J., and W. Powderly. 2004. Chapter 77–Papillomavirus. In: *Infectious Disease.* 2nd ed. Philadelphia: Mosby, 829.

Diaz, L. 2008. Human papilloma virus–prevention and treatment. *Obstetrics and Gynecology Clinics* 35(2):199–217.

Erb, T. and R. Beigi. 2008. Update on infectious diseases in adolescent gynecology. *J. Ped. Adol. Gyn.* 21(3). www.mdconsult.com/das/article/body/180373429-3/jorg=journal+source=MI+sp=2.

Ferency, A., and E. Franco. 2007. HPV: Answering your worried patients' questions. *Contemporary Ob/Gyn.* 52(4):48–54.

Forhan, S. E., et al. 2009. Prevalence of sexually transmitted infections among female adolescents aged 14-19 in the United States. *Pediatrics* 124(6): 1505-1512.

Frenkl, T., and J. Potts. 2008. Sexually transmitted infections. *Urol. Clin. North Am.* 35(1):33–46. www.mdconsult.com/das/article/body/179880626-6/jorg=journal&source=MI7sp=2-196586&sid=943626543/N/619999/1.html?issn=0094-1043.

Johnny, S., and R. Ho. 2005. Strengthening linkages for student success. API Teen Outreach, Asian and Pacific Islander Hepatitis B Task Force. www.cdc.gov/hepatitis/Resources/MtgsConf/NatVHPrevConc2005/Tuesday/A1-Johnny.pdf.

Shetty, A., and Y. Maldonado. 2008. Chapter 109–Epidemiology and prevention of HIV infection in children and adolescents. In: *Principles and Practice of Pediatric Infectious Diseases,* S. Long, ed. 3rd ed., Philadelphia: Churchill Livingstone. www.mdconsult. com/das/book/body/180926217-21/0/1679/113.html?tocnode= 55242292&fromURL=113.html#4-u1.0-B978-0-443-06687-0.. X5001-2—section22_2301.

Yen S., and A. Tolani A. 2009. Websites mislead teens about sexual health. *Ob/Gyn News.* 44(8):32.

Chapter 5

Albert, B. 2007. With one voice: America's adults and teens sound off about teen pregnancy. www.thenationalcampaign.org/resources/ pdf/pubs/WOV2007_fulltext.pdf.

American College of Obstetricians and Gynecologists. The Initial Reproductive Health Visit. Committee Opinion. No. 598, 2014.

American College of Obstetricians and Gynecologists. 2008. Rise in births to teens worrisome—ACOG encourages support of the National Day to Prevent Teen Pregnancy. www.acog.org/from_ home/publications/press_releases/nr05-01-08-1.cfm.

Centers for Disease Control and Prevention. 2010. National STD Prevention Conference. Most teens not provided STD or pregnancy prevention counseling during checkups. www.cdc.gov/ stdconference/2000/media/Teens2000.htm.

Communication and Conflict. Principles of effective interpersonal communication. www.communicationandconflict.com.

Eaton, D. K., et al. 2009. Youth risk behavior surveillance—United States 2009. Centers for Disease Control and Prevention. www. cdc.gov/mmwr/PDF/ss/ss5905.pdf.

Family Education Network. 2000. Increasing communication between parent and teenager. www.life.familyeducation.com/teen/communication/39355.html.

Focus Adolescent Services. 2000. How can parents model good listening skills? www.focusas.com/ListeningSkills.html.

How to be an active parent. The Oprah Winfrey Show. 2002. www.oprah.com/relationships/How-to-Be-an-Active-Parent.

Kirby, D. 2007. Research findings on programs to reduce teen pregnancy and STDs. www.thenationalcampaign.org/resources/pdf/pubs/EA2007_FINAL.pdf.

Rudder, D. B. 2008. The teen brain: a work in progress. Harvardmagazine.com/2008/the-teen-brain.html.

SMHAI. 2004. How to be a good listener. suicideandmentalhealthassociationinternational.org/howgoodlisten.html.

Chapter 6

Advocates for Youth. 2009. Adolescent sexual health in Europe and the United States: why the difference? www.advocatesforyouth.org/index.php?option=com_content&task=view&id=419&Itemid=177.

Albert, B. 2004. With one voice: America's adults and teens sound off about teen pregnancy, an annual national survey. Washington, DC: The National Campaign to Prevent Teen Pregnancy, 2004.

Ali. L., and J. Scelfo. 2002. Choosing virginity. *Newsweek.* December 9:61–71.

Avert.org Abstinence and sex education. www.avert.org/abstinence.htm.

Espey, E. 2007. Family planning American style: why it's so hard to control birth in the US. *Ob. Gyn. Clin.* 34(1):1–17.

Finer, L. B. 2007. Trends in premarital sex in the United States, 1954–2003. *Public Health Reports.* 122:73–78.

Interview with Judith Clark, Executive Director, Hawaii Youth Services Network, November 2009.

Jemmott, J., et al. 2010. Efficacy of a theory-based abstinence-only intervention over 24 months. *Arch. Ped. Adol. Med.* 164(2):152–159.

Masland, M. Carnal knowledge: The sex ed debate. www.msnbc.msn.com/id/3071001/544329.asp.

National Campaign to Prevent Teen Pregnancy. 2005. The cautious generation: teens having less sex and using contraception more. www.thenationalcampaign.org/about-us/PDF/Spring2005update.pdf.

———. 2006. New research shows that teens with religious parents and friends are more likely to delay sexual activity. www.thenationalcampaign.org/about-us/PDF/Winter2006update.pdf.

———. Faith matters: how African-American faith communities can help prevent teen pregnancy. www.thenationalcampaign.org/resources/pdf/pubs/FaithMatters_FINAL.pdf.

Ott, M. 2007. Counseling teens about abstinence. *J. Ped. Gyn.* 20(1):39–44.

Chapter 7

American College of Obstetricians and Gynecologists. Adolescents and Long-Acting Reversible Contraception: Implants and Intrauterine Devices. Committee Opinion No. 539 (Reaffirmed 2014).

_____. Emergency Contraception. Practice Bulletin No. 152, 2015.

Allan Guttmacher Institute. 2010. Facts on American teens' sexual and reproductive health. www.guttmacher.org/pubs/FB-ATSRH.html.

———. 2008. Facts on contraceptive use. www.guttmacher.org/pubs/fb_contr_use.html.

———. 2001. Teenagers' sexual and reproductive health: developed countries. www.guttmacher.org/pubs/fb_teens.html.

Albert, B. 2007. With one voice: America's adults and teens sound off about teen pregnancy. www.thenationalcampaign.org/resources/pdf/pubs/WOV2007_fulltext.pdf.

American Academy of Family Physicians. Contraception, First Consult, MD Consult. www.aafp.org.

Centers for Disease Control and Prevention. 2010. Morbidity and mortality weekly report. U.S. medical eligibility criteria for contraceptive use. www.cdc.gov/mmwr/pdf/rr/rr59e0528.pdf.

———. 2010. Progress Review Focus Area 9-Family Planning Presentation. www.cdc.gov/nchs/ppt/hp2010/focus_areas/fa09_2_ppt/fa09_fp2_ppt.htm.

Daniels, K., et al. 2015. Contraceptive Methods Women Have Ever Used: United States, 1982-2011. *National Health Statistics Reports* 62, February 2015.

Eaton, D. K., et al. 2009. Youth risk behavior surveillance—United States 2009. Centers for Disease Control and Prevention. www.cdc.gov/mmwr/PDF/ss/ss5905.pdf.

English, A. 2000. Reproductive health care for adolescents, critical legal issues. *Obstetrics & Gynecology* 27(1):195–211.

Feldman, E. 2006. Contraceptive care for the adolescent. *Primary Care: Clinics in Office Practice* 33(2):405–31.

Guttmacher Institute. An Overview of Minors' Consent Law. State Policies in Brief, as of January 2016.

Isley, M., and A. Edelman. 2007. Contraceptive implants: an overview and update. Obstetrical and Gyn Clinics 34(1):73–90.

Lara-Torre, E. 2009. Update in adolescent contraception. *Obstetrics and Gynecology Clinics* 35(1):119-128.

Leeman, L. 2007. Medical barriers to effective contraception. *Obstetrics and Gynecology Clinics* 34(1):19-29.

Lemay, C. A., et al. 2007. Adolescent mothers' attitudes toward contraceptive use before and after pregnancy. *J. Ped. Adol. Gyn.* 20(4):233–40.

Lerand, S. J. 2007. Teach the teacher: adolescent confidentiality and minors' consent. *J. Ped. Adol. Gyn.* 20(6):377–80.

Lerand, S. J., et al. 2007. Communication with our teens: associations between confidential service and parent-teen communication. *J. Ped. Adol. Gyn.* 20(3):173–8.

Prine, L. 2007. Emergency contraception, myths and facts. *Ob. Gyn.* 34(1):127–36.

Reddy, D. M., R. Fleming, and C. Swain. 2002. Effect of mandatory parental notification on adolescent girls' use of sexual health care services. *JAMA* 288:710–714.

Shulman, L., and M. Gilliam. 2003. Improving contraceptive use among adolescents. *Dialogues in Contraception* 7(8):1–4.

Woods, J. L., et al. 2009. Contraceptive withdrawal in adolescents: A complex picture of usage. *J. Ped. Adol. Gyn.* 22(4):233-237.

Chapter 8

American Academy of Pediatrics. 2012. Circumcision Policy Statement. *Pediatrics* 130, Issue 3.

American College of Obstetricians and Gynecologists. Cervical Cancer Screening and Prevention. Practice Bulletin No. 157, 2016.

———. Human Papillomavirus Vaccination. Committee Opinion No. 641, 2015.

Articles Base. 2009. Celebrities who don't drink alcohol. www.articlesbase.com/art-and-entertainment-articles/celebrities-who-don't-drink-alcohol.

Boschert, S. 2008. Most teen girls lack knowledge of STIs. *Ob/Gyn News* (43)18:14.

Braverman, P. K. 2006. Body art: piercing, tattooing, and scarification. *Adolescent Medical Clinics* 17(3):505–19.

Bullock, L. 2008. CDC pleased with rate of teens getting HPV vaccine. *Ob/Gyn News.* (43)21:1.

Centers for Disease Control and Prevention. Hepatitis B FAQs for the public. www.cdc.gov/hepatitis/B/bFAQ.htm.

———. HIV testing among adolescents. www.cdc.gov/healthyyouth/sexualbehaviors/pdf/hivtesting-adolescents.

———. 2010. HPV vaccine: what you need to know. www.cdc.gov/vaccines/pubs/VIS/downloads/vis-hpv-gardasil.pdf.

————. 2008. Male circumcision and risk for HIV transmission and other health conditions: implications for the United States. www.cdc.gov/hiv/resources/factsheets/circumcision.htm.

————. 2014. Pre-Exposure Prophylaxis (PrEP) for HIV Infection. www.cdc.gov/hiv/pdf/PrEP_fact_sheet_final.pdf.

————. 2009. Provisional recommendations for HPV vaccine. ACIP (Advisory Committee on Immunization Practices). www.cdc.gov/vaccines/recs/provisional/downloads/hpv-vac-dec2009-508.pdf.

————. Questions & answers for parents of pre-teens about human papillomavirus (HPV) and the HPV vaccine. www.cdc.gov/vaccines/spec-grps/preteens-adol/07gallery/downloads/f_qahpv_parents_pr.pdf.

Child Trends. 2003. Safer choices. www.childtrends.org/Lifecourse/programs/saferchoices.htm.

Diaz, M. 2008. Humanpapilloma virus—prevention and treatment. *Obstetrics and Gynecology Clinics* 35(2):199–217.

Disney Dreaming. 2009. Taylor Swift doesn't use drugs or alcohol to rebel. www.disneydreaming.com/2009/05/14/taylor-swift-doesn't-use-drugs-or-alcohol-to-rebel.

Federal Drug Administration News Release. 2014. FDA approves Gardasil 9 for prevention of certain cancers caused by five additional types of HPV. www.fda.gov/NewsEvents/Newsroom/PressAnnouncements/ucm426485.htm

Hepatitis B Foundation. Hepatitis B vaccine—prevention measures. www.hepb.org/professionals/prevention_measures.htm.

Merck & Co., Inc. 2009. Information from FDA and CDC on the safety of GARDASIL, human papillomavirus quadrivalent (types

6, 11, 16, 18) vaccine, recombinant. www.gardasil.com/what-is-gardasil/information-on-gardasil.

Merck & Co., Inc. 2009. Merck is pleased the FDA and CDC re-affirm the safety profile of Gardasil [human papillomavirus quadrivalent (types 6, 11, 16 and 18) vaccine, recombinant]. www.merck.com/newsroom/news-release-archive/product/2009_0820.html.

Pelton, S. 2008. What we know about Gardasil's adverse events. *Ob/ Gyn News* 43(20):9.

Science Daily. 2008. Teens who repeatedly cut themselves have greater HIV risk. www.sciencedaily.com/releases/2008/06/080612070410.htm.

Splete, H. 2008. Safety tops parents' concerns on HPV vaccine. *Ob/ Gyn News* (43)18:9.

*For more details on a reference, email drsheilaoverton@gmail.com

Printed in the United States
By Bookmasters